The Age of the Clans

The Highlands from Somerled to the Clearances

Robert Dodgshon

Series editor: Gordon Barclay

BIRLINN

with

HISTORIC SCOTLAND

Copyright © Robert Dodgshon, 2002

Illustrations © Robert Dodgshon, unless otherwise stated

British Library Cataloguing-in-Publication data

A catalogue record for this book is available on request from the British Library

ISBN 1 84158 144 5

First published by Birlinn Ltd

West Newington House, 10 Newington Road, Edinburgh EH9 1QS

British Library Cataloguing-in-Publication Data

A catalogue record for this book is available on request
from the British Library

Typesetting and design by Carnegie Publishing Ltd, Lancaster

Printed and bound in Spain by Book Print SL

Contents

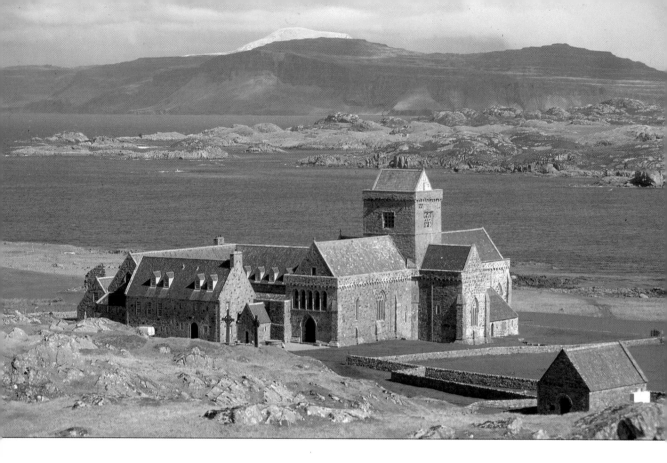

The World of Somerled

Though Malcolm I and his successors called themselves kings of the Scots, and laid claim to much of Scotland, a mid-twelfth-century seer trying to foretell the history of the Highlands and Islands might have been forgiven if he or she despaired of the number of outcomes that still seemed possible. Different parts of the region were under the control of different groups, each of whom would have harboured ambitions to secure the whole. The main body of the Highlands was still in the control of Gaelic lords and earls. In parts of the eastern and northern Highlands, remnants of a deep-rooted Pictish aristocracy still resided, though now Gaelicised. In the far north and in the Outer Hebrides, powerful vassals of the Norse king held power, with the Earl of Orkney holding sway in the north and the King of Mann and the Isles holding sway in the Outer Hebrides. In the south-west Highlands and Islands lay the sprawling powerbase of Somerled Macgillebrigte, a powerful, independent lord who had roots in Gaelic society, as well as links to the Norse. Referred to in some sources as not just lord but king of Argyll, he commanded a territory that embraced most of modern-day Argyll together with Moidart and Knoydart.

Feudalism and the Highlands

The crowning of David I as King of Scots introduced a powerful new element into the equation. Brought up in southern England, his vision was of a thoroughly feudalised Scotland in which the Crown exercised superiority over all men and all land, with the major landholders swearing allegiance to the king as his vassals and holding their land from him in return for military service. In turn, these landholders sublet their land to those who worked the soil in return for labour services and food rents. An essential part of David I's strategy was the planting of Anglo-Norman knights and families on estates confiscated from Scottish landholders. Overnight, control over the landscape and its inhabitants passed into the hands of the Crown and its vassals and became part of the way the Crown controlled the Scottish realm. In addition to planting new Anglo-Norman families across southern and central Scotland, David I also planted new families around the eastern and southern edges of the Highlands. Families who were to play a key role in Highland history, like the Stewarts, Moray and Menzies, were amongst them, but some existing Gaelic landowners in this area acknowledged the political realities that now confronted them by swearing allegiance to the Crown and being regranted their estates from the Crown.

Anglo-Norman feudalism was a system that acquired stability only through its continuous expansion. The need for this expansion came from the way in which Anglo-Norman lords and knights passed their estates to a single son. As a result, extra land had to be found for those sons who were not provided for by these family settlements. The problem was that, by the mid-twelfth century, the frontier for Anglo-Norman expansion had reached the Scottish Highlands. As an environment, the region was neither suited to the kind of warfare that fully armoured knights excelled at nor could the local environment sustain their heavy maintenance costs. Further, when it came to the western seaboard, power depended on one's maritime capability. Those who knew the local tides and races intimately always had a tactical advantage over better equipped navies unfamiliar with its seas and coasts. For these reasons, once the Scottish Crown looked to penetrate deep into the Highlands, its best option was always to build alliances with local lords and to use these alliances to coerce those who were less compliant.

Early Clans

The spread of Crown feudalism under these conditions was a long drawn-out affair, full of compromises to local circumstances and hints of what the 8th Duke of Argyll called 'clan feudalism', with kin ties being as strong as those between lord and vassal. Indeed, for much of

the medieval and early modern periods, we can divide the region into areas where Crown authority held sway and areas where it did not, with the Crown continually struggling to change the balance between the two. Exploiting moments of weakness was the key to its strategy. One such moment presented itself in 1164. In contrast to the rule of primogeniture amongst his Anglo-Norman neighbours, Somerled's vast territory was divided between his three 'surviving' sons, Dugald and Ranald and Angus, following his death in 1164. Dugald had Lorne, Benderloch and Lismore, the core and most fertile part of Somerled's territory. Ranald acquired the southern and western territories, namely Islay, Jura, Kintyre, Morvern and Ardnamurchan, whilst Angus was given the northern territories or Gormoran. The MacSorleys, as the decendants of Somerled were collectively called, have an important place in Highland history because they developed into clans that dominated the west Highlands and Islands for the next 3–400 years: the Macdougalls, Macdonalds, Clanranalds and MacRuairis. These were not necessarily the first clans in the Highlands, but they were certainly amongst the earliest that we can document in any detail. The rivalry amongst them, and with others around them, over the control of territory shaped the highly dynamic and volatile character of clans over the next 3–400 years. A saga called the *King's Mirror* captured these qualities in the dramatic phrase: 'where boundaries of the territories of the chiefs touch, he places a moving wheel on a restless axle'. It was precisely because the power of lords like Somerled was personal rather than in any way constitutional that events like his death could trigger such struggles.

'a moving wheel on a restless axle'

In fact, the decomposition of Somerled's lordship was not straightforward. The different branches of the MacSorleys, especially those descended from Dugald and Ranald, competed vigorously. Others exploited the instability of the moment to redraw the map of power at a larger scale. The Scottish Crown saw the break-up of Somerled's great lordship as an opportunity to press its authority over the region and to draw it more emphatically within the Scottish realm. Godfrey, the Norse king, also saw it as the opportunity for restoring Norse control in the southern Hebrides. Positioning himself, he took direct control over the existing Norse territories in the Outer Hebrides and Skye. By 1195, after curbing the power of the Earl of

A Medieval Galley

Being able to move fighting men quickly and easily around the west coast was essential for those who wished to control the western seaboard. Powerful lords set land in return for the maintenance of galleys with so-many oars. Robert the Bruce, for example, granted land in Kilninver in 1313 for the service of a ship with 26 oars. Others, like MacLeod of MacLeod, can be found giving a galley in payment of brideprice. Rorie MacLeod, for instance, gave 'ane gailley of twentie foure airis with her sailling and rowing gear gud and sufficient' to John Moydart, son of the Captain of Clanranald, when John married his daughter in 1613.

CHRIS BROWN

Orkney by taking direct control over Shetland, he had established the means to mount expeditions to the west of Scotland without hinder.

Fuelled by the convergence of these conflicting ambitions, the century or so following Somerled's death formed a turbulent period for the western Highlands and Islands. Much of the conflict was focused on the territory of Somerled's former lordship. Within Somerled's former lordship itself, the MacSorleys fought with each other in struggles over dominance, the Macdougalls and Macdonalds tending to take different sides in any wider political dispute. In southern Argyll, tensions arose where the Macdonalds, a key branch of the MacSorleys, confronted newly planted Anglo-Norman families like the Stewarts. To the north, the MacRuairi branch of the MacSorleys routinely fought with the alliances of Norse clans that were grouped together as the Godfreysons and who controlled Skye and the Outer Hebrides, though by the mid-thirteenth century, the MacRuairi chief can be found working with the Norse king and using every opportunity to confront the Scottish king.

In 1263, fearful that the Scottish king, Alexander III, might be about to seize the Hebrides, the Norse king, Haakon IV, led an expeditionary force to the Western Isles. Drawn south, some of his men were routed at Largs when they tried to recover goods from ships that had been damaged in a storm. Sensing the weakness of his position, Haakon retreated north only to die soon after in Shetland. As with Somerled, his death marked a significant point in the history of the region for his successor quickly reached a peace with Alexander III and, by the Treaty of Perth, 1266, ceded the Hebrides to him. Yet despite the Treaty, the Scottish Crown subsequently exercised only a nominal lordship over the Hebrides. Indeed, it spent the next three or four centuries trying to turn its authority over the region into hard reality.

Highland Strongholds

The twelfth and thirteenth centuries left a durable legacy of their turbulent conditions. Across the region, numerous stone-built castles were built. Their number highlights the extent to which this was a period in which securing one's defence was a paramount claim on resources at least for those who held the political reins. Significantly, it was a claim on the resources not just of those who upheld the interests of the Scottish Crown, but also of those to the west and north who saw themselves as still exercising a Gaelic or Norse lordship. In distribution, they were spread widely, with strongholds built within the main body of the Highlands as well as around its edges. What particularly impresses is the relatively heavy concentration of castles that appeared along the western seaboard and across the islands of the west. These defined a very active frontier zone, initially between the

Castle Sween, Argyll
HISTORIC SCOTLAND

Scottish and Norse Crowns, but later between the Scottish Crown and the Lordship of the Isles, an area in which rival power blocs repeatedly pressed against each other like moving tectonic plates.

In style, these early castles comprised a massive but simple lime and stone enclosure or curtain wall. Some were rectangular in shape others circular and as much as 30–40 metres in diameter. Some reinforced their defensive qualities by using a rock outcrop (eg Dunstaffnage) or even an island site. Others had corner towers added for extra defence. Living quarters, kitchens and workshops were provided by timber-framed buildings arranged around the inner edge of the enclosure. In a landscape in which most ordinary peasants lived in small turf or stone-based huts, such large stone-girt enclosures must have expressed all the standing and authority of lords and chiefs in the most tangible and visible way.

Ecclesiastical Landscapes

Stone-built castles of enclosure were not the only monuments to appear during the twelfth and thirteenth centuries that were built to last. These centuries also witnessed the construction of stone-based ecclesiastical buildings, ranging from monastic sites down to humble chapels. The most significant was undoubtedly the Benedictine abbey established at Iona *c* 1200, the abbey's stone church replacing the timber-framed buildings that had characterised the site since Columba first established his monastery on the site back in the sixth century AD. In a region greatly afflicted by warring, such a foundation was inevitably aided by those who controlled the area. In the case of Iona, it was Somerled's son, Reginald, now a powerful lord in his own right, controlling Islay and Kintyre. It was the second monastic foundation Reginald had supported for he had probably helped his father to establish Saddell Abbey, Kintyre, a decade or so earlier. The example set was followed by others, such as the Macdougal family, who founded the priory at Ardchattan in 1230.

Though these monastic centres were easily the most striking manifestation of the new fashion for building churches in stone, they were not the only examples. Across the region many lesser churches and chapels were built or rebuilt using the skills of the mason as well as the carpenter. At the outset, these stone-set churches were small, rectangular buildings, with no internal subdivisions. The smallest were barely 15 metres in length, the largest around 20–25 metres, though some were subsequently extended lengthwise. In the western parts of the region, some of the stone-set churches and chapels that appeared during this period may have replaced a denser, more localised pattern of chapels, so that their construction may have been bound up as much with changes in ecclesiastical organisation as in the style of churches. The spread of the parish system over the 12th and 13th centuries, with its local centralisation of religious provision, provides an obvious source of this organisational change. However, we need to be mindful of the wider context. Examples of new, more substantial churches appeared across the region during the 12th and 13th centuries, both in areas of Gaelic and Norse lordship and in those parts firmly under the control of the Scottish Crown.

The spread of a new parochial system is unlikely to have crossed such boundaries in a smooth, uninterrupted way and we need to keep other reasons for the building of stone-built chapels in mind. A contributory factor may have been changes in the availability of timber. Recent work has highlighted the extent to which available woodland, at least along parts of the western seaboard, began to decline significantly from AD 1000. However, the depletion of timber supplies was too variable across the region to provide an easy explanation for the shift into stone. Indeed, most Hebridean islands are unlikely to have had a ready supply of timber for church building long before the twelfth century. More relevant as a general context is the fact that the twelfth and thirteenth centuries formed the medieval climatic optimum, a phase of warmer conditions. For the ordinary peasant, this was a time when both crops and animals thrived, harvests failed less often and the landscape filled out with more settlements and more tenants. Landlords must have gathered in far more as tribute or rent, filling their girnal houses, or foodstores, to excess. The greater surpluses so gathered would have supported the building of stone-set castles and churches.

St Mary's Abbey, Iona
HISTORIC SCOTLAND

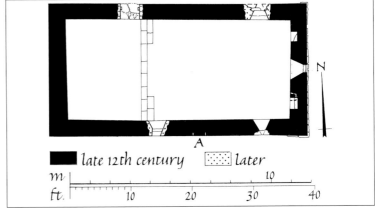

Early stone-built chapel.
Medieval chapel and plan, Keills, Knapdale.
CROWN COPYRIGHT/RCAHMS

What Lies Hidden?

Both archaeological and documentary sources have far less to say about the great bulk of Highland society, those who inhabited and worked the farming townships of Somerled's world. Some have tried to fill this gap by drawing on stereotypes that stress the prehistoric roots of the farming township and its resilience to change, so that what appears in detail in the eighteenth century, with its runrig organisation of landholding and its infield-outfield cropping of land, is made to speak for earlier periods like the 12th and 13th centuries. Such an approach effectively freezes the life of townships, stripping away their experience of history and its succession of military struggles, political changes, subsistence crises, climatic shifts, and so on. As in other parts of Europe, we must expect the 12th and 13th centuries to have been a time of vigorous population growth and settlement expansion, with communities busy creating new areas of arable and new townships.

Chiefs and Clansmen

What was a Clan?

Though clans are popularly seen as bonded together by ties of kinship, in reality, they were much more diverse in character. This was especially true of the larger clans. At the core of any clan was always a dominant family. As this family expanded and acquired more land, it invariably became divided into a number of different family segments known as *sliochdan*, each of which was associated with a different portion of the territory held by the family. As the clan expanded, it maintained a careful genealogical record of its descent from the ancestor founder after whom it was named and of when each branch or *sliochd* separated out from the main family stem. Branches became ranked according to when they first established themselves as a separate *sliochd*. But whether a family established itself as a separate branch of a clan depended as much on whether it acquired the land for itself as on its kinship connections with the founder of the clan. For this reason, the branches into which clans became divided were invariably identified by the territory with which they were associated, so that a clan like the Clanranald Macdonalds was divided into branches like the Macdonalds of Glengarry or the Macdonalds of Knoydart.

This need to acquire land meant that clans were always seeking to be expansive. Different strategies were open to them. Some clans claimed to hold land on the point of a sword, constantly pushing out aggressively against weaker rival clans. With the spread of feudalism, though, clans came to hold land by charter from the Crown. Those who gained most by this were those who professed Crown loyalty or served its interests. Indeed, by far the most dramatic changes in landholding and, ultimately, clan geography were precipitated by Crown confiscation and reallocation of land. But whether they held land on the point of a sword or by Crown charter, many rival clans competed strongly over disputed territories, harassing and, on occasion, even murdering each other's tenants to further their claims. Marriage was used to bolster their aspirations further, the more successful conserving land by marrying their women within the clan and acquiring more land by marrying off their men to the heiresses of other clans. Once land was acquired, clans strove to fill it with clansmen if not kinsmen. What impresses is the extent to which they were willing to settle on marginal land or on islands that were difficult to access for much of the year simply because having control over land, any sort of land, was essential if a new branch of the clan was to establish itself. A clan without land was seen as a broken clan.

Forms of Identity

The way in which individuals identified themselves in traditional Highland society could take different forms. Chiefs were identified as the chiefs of this or that clan, or associated with their territory, like the Campbells of Argyll or of Glenorchy. In large complex clans, like the Campbells, the heads of the different segments were identified through the different territories that they controlled, so that the identity of the clan became closely mapped into the space that it occupied. At lower social levels, identity took a different form. When we look through charters dealing with mundane matters like rentals, individuals were identified through their patronyms. In most cases, they represented themselves three-generationally. Rorie McEan VcLachlane, for example, a tenant listed in the township of Belgerbay, South Uist, in 1692 was Rorie, son of Ian, grandson of Lachlan. However, we also find many examples of individuals who extended their patronymic identity back four generations, and less frequently, even beyond, such as Rannald McEan VcCuil VcCowin who was listed in the same 1692 rental as a tenant in Bowisdale. Alongside the use of patronyms, we also find the use of clan names. Individuals tended to use their patronym within the context of the local community and their clan name when they were dealing with the wider world.

Family Tree of Campbell of Glenorchy

All Highland clans maintained genealogies
as a matter of course. Many were highly
contrived, emphasising some links more
than others or fabricating links where it
served their interest. Initially, most
genealogies were memorised by official clan
historians and only came to be written
down towards the end of the medieval
period or later. Few could aspire to the very
literal portrayal of family links depicted in
the painting of the Campbell of Glenorchy's
family tree by George Jamesone, 1635. The
family that was planting great trees in the
grounds around Taymouth from the early
eighteenth century onwards was symbolised
in the painting as the greatest tree of all.
NATIONAL GALLERIES OF SCOTLAND

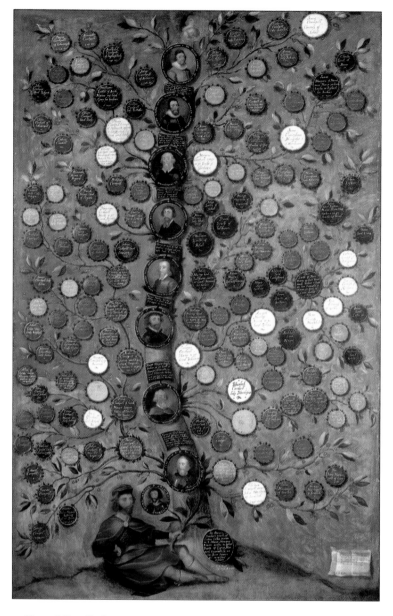

Yet whilst all clans maintained genealogies as a matter of course, at
least for the ties that bound the leading lineages or *sliochdan*, and whilst
they presented themselves to the wider world as communities of
kinsmen, it does not follow that all those who regarded themselves as
members of a particular clan were bound together by real ties of
kinship. Once we move beyond their leading families, the bonds that
tied most clans of any size became as much based on presumed ties of
kin as on real ties. To understand this point, we need to appreciate
how clans were organised. Usually, the leading families or *sliochdan*
controlled different portions of the clan's territory either because they
acted as tacksmen for the clan chief, or held it as property in their

own right. A tacksman was someone given the tack or lease of a district and who was responsible for subletting its townships to those who tilled the soil, but tacksmen also had a vital military and political role, exercising control over the district in the interests of the clan. By using its senior families in this way, a clan could impose its genealogical stamp over a large extended territory. However, it was very easy for a successful clan to acquire land quicker than it could breed new tenants to occupy it, with its grasp of territory exceeding its biological success as a family. As a result, when we get down to

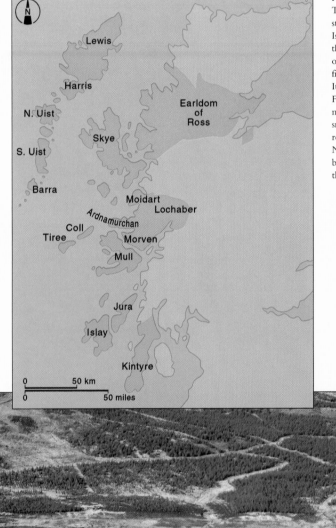

Finlaggan

The Lordship of the Isles was an alliance of lordship that stretched across the Western Isles and adjacent mainland, from Islay to Lewis. The first person to assume the title of Lord of the Isles was John of Islay, a grandson of Donald, the founder of the Clan Donald, and a descendant of Somerled. Emerging first in the 1340s, the Lordship lasted until its collapse in 1493. Its centre was on two small islands at the east end of Loch Finlaggan on Islay, islands that were linked together and to the mainland by a causeway. One part of the site was occupied by a small cluster of buildings, the most important of which was a rectangular structure that functioned as a hall and a chapel. Nearby, on the adjacent island, are the remains of another building that served as the meeting house for the Council of the Isles.

PHOTOGRAPHS:
DAVID CALDWELL

those who actually farmed the land, those who held mere fractions of a township (such as one-third, or one-eighth) or simply a cottage, we find more complex patterns of kinship. Many would have been individuals who had no genuine ties of kinship to a clan, but who, nevertheless, claimed themselves as members of the landowner's clan simply because it improved their claim on land. In some cases, families and lesser clans faked their genealogy so as to legitimise their assumptions of kinship.

Another solution to the problem of living in the shadow of a dominant clan was to contract a bond of manrent with them, an agreement whereby individuals and their families aligned themselves with a dominant clan. This was widely used by the Campbells of Glenorchy to extend their sway over the lesser families around them. Another way in which expansive clans could reach beyond themselves during the late medieval period was by drawing up a bond of friendship or alliance with another clan chief, a bond that committed each clan to treat the other 'as if they were kin' and to fight in each other's cause.

Thus, a bond of 1521 between Alexander MacDuan MacAlister of Glengarry and Donald Ewen Allanson of Lochiel pledged them to defend each other's interest and to lease land to each other's kin if they obtained it.

To understand why clans were based on assumed as well as on genuine ties of kinship, we also need to look at the context in which they operated. Clans arose in areas where the power of central authority was weak. At one extreme, they provided a form of DIY power structure, one put together by force of arms and circumstance, with chiefs holding their land on what they saw as the point of a sword. At the other, they provided a means by which the Crown, through its increasing control over Highland lords and chiefs, could bring its authority to bear on particular areas. In either case, clans provided a mantle of authority. By attaching themselves to

Bond of Manrent
A bond of manrent between Donald Pettie in Ardetie and Duncan Campbell of Glenorchy lying over an extract from a 1595 rental.

a clan, whether their attachment was based on real ties of kinship or not, individuals conformed to the prevailing political order of an area.

Clans though, were not stable institutions. They competed fiercely over territory. At any one point, we can find successful clans expanding and failing clans in retreat. This was one reason why clan geography was a complex fluid affair, not easily mapped. When a clan gained possession of a new area, such as when the Campbells of Argyll acquired control over Mull and Tiree during the seventeenth century, displacing MacLeans in the process, it asserted control by moving in new tacksmen and doing so quickly. Filling their townships with tenants who were loyal clansmen was a longer, slower business. It is in these circumstances that we find individuals assuming a new clan identity, aligning themselves with changes in the political landscape in order to maintain their grip on land. But such switches of identity were not always so straightforward. Some of the most persistent feuds in the region stemmed from the conflict that arose from the mismatch of loyalties between the clan that controlled land and those who occupied it.

Building Chiefly Status

The head of a clan was its chief, though in large and complex clans, the head of a branch could also be styled as a chief, albeit a lesser one to the chief who ruled over the clan as a whole. The most notable example of this sort of ranking was the elaborate hierarchy of chiefs that developed around the Lordship of the Isles from its initial formation in the mid-fourteenth century down to its collapse in 1493. The status of a clan was embodied in that of its chief. All chiefs set out to enhance their status and that of their clan both through the acquisition of more land and through display behaviour. These two forms of status enhancement were intimately linked. The more land controlled by a chief, then the more clansmen he could settle as tenants and the more rent he could uplift and use to build status.

Though some cash payments had started to appear by the sixteenth century, the traditional rent bundle of the Highland landowner was made up of rent payments in kind, primarily grain, livestock and livestock produce, but also including payments as varied as poultry, fish, whisky and cloth. Inevitably, those chiefs who acquired fertile land, such as on Islay or in Netherlorne, could accumulate more grain in their girnal houses or stock in their bowhouses than those who had access to poorer land, such as in Knoydart. Easily the most prized item of rent for any would-be chief was cattle. It is no coincidence that the focal point for the Lordship of the Isles, Finlaggan, lay at the centre of an area rated for its production of cattle. Nor should we be surprised at the way early marriage contracts involved the payment of cattle as brideprice, a payment made by the bride's family to the groom.

Much of the character of the clan system derived from how chiefs used their rent payments in kind to enhance their status. A number of possibilities were open to them. The most tangible symbol of consumption was the sort of residence that a chief built for himself. Chiefs with any sort of pretension looked to build a fortified dwelling, either a castle or simple tower house. The castles of enclosure that had appeared by the 12th and 13th centuries had, by the 14th and 15th centuries, begun to acquire more elaborate defences, with corner towers, wings, and more secure entrances. Domestic quarters too were developed, with the timber-framed buildings or two-storey stone dwellings that had characterised early castles of enclosure being replaced, or extended upwards, with the building of three- or four-storey tower houses inside or beside their curtain walls. Other lesser chiefs built free-standing

Tower House

Tower house, Breacachadh Castle, Coll.

tower houses, whose stark towering walls must have added their own psychology of rank to a landscape otherwise dominated by low, temporary dwellings. This investment in castles or fortified tower houses provided protection in what was an unsettled, warring society, one striven by disputes and feuds that lasted for centuries and in which the distinction between clans loyal to the Crown and those antagonistic to it was simply another basis of dispute in a society already replete with them. In use though, castles and tower houses also served as a focus for a range of chiefly display behaviour.

Innis Chonnell Castle, Argyll, *circa* **late fifteenth century**

The earliest castles were castles of enclosure. In their simplest form, they consisted of a thick curtain wall, elaborated by a series of timber-framed buildings along part of its inner edge. In time, they were further elaborated by the addition of corner towers and tower houses. The combined effect of these changes can be seen in the reconstruction of Innis Chonnell Castle, Argyll. Occupying a small island beside the eastern shore of Loch Awe, Innis Chonnell formed the original stronghold of the Campbells of Argyll. It began as a rectangular castle of enclosure, elaborated by one or two simple corner towers, that was erected in the thirteenth century. This enclosure formed the inner bailey. Living and service quarters were provided by a cluster of buildings located around the edge of the inner bailey. During the early fifteenth century, the core of the site was modified with the construction of a new tower in the south-west corner of the inner bailey, and a range of buildings, of which the most significant was a four-storeyed block that included a hall on the first floor. The middle and outer baileys were probably in existence by this point so that the entire castle probably had the appearance depicted above. Soon after, though, Colin Campbell, the first Earl of Argyll, moved the family's principal residence to Inveraray. Innis Chonnell continued in use as a residence for successive captains of Innis Chonnell down to the start of the eighteenth century, when it was finally abandoned.
CHRIS BROWN

MacLeod's Tables, Skye
For the chief of MacLeod, the flat tops of MacLeod's Tables formed the ideal backcloth for Dunvegan Castle. The symbolism of such a name was obvious to all who gazed at them. Any chief with a table this large, especially a table that was inextricably part of the natural order, must be a great chief because he could feast and host on a lavish scale.

Central to this display behaviour was the role of the castle or tower house as a stage for feasting and displays of hospitality. In an environment in which scarcity was recurrent, nothing boosted a chief's status more than his command over the surpluses of food and its conspicuous consumption via occasional bouts of feasting. Indeed, for those who tilled the land and herded the stock, providing food for their chief and his table were seen to have the first claim on the produce of the land. Even if it was only a myth, the story that early charters for the Macdonald of the Isles contained the phrase that tenants should provide food for Macdonald's table before all else was a powerful statement about the social order that underpinned the clan system.

Feastings were occasions of special celebration, such as a marriage or the inauguration of a new chief. As well as guests, they involved the chief's household men. The latter were a diverse group, comprising members of the chief's bodyguard, a group made up of men from the leading lineages, and the chief's retainers: such as his piper, harpist, the clan story-teller or historian and even, in the case of MacLeod of MacLeod, his fool. In most cases, particular families held these positions on an hereditary basis. Successive generations of the MacDuffie or MacPhie family of Colonsay, for instance, were record-keepers for the Lord of the Isles. Likewise, the MacIlschenachs were his hereditary harpists. When we look through estate rentals, we find that these specialist retainers often had a holding rent-free or for a token rent in return for their services, the service and holding remaining in the hands of a family for generations. As late as 1718, for instance, the township of Sterigally on South Uist was held rent-free by the MacMhuirichs for 'Registring the Deeds & Geneologies of the family [=the Captain of Clanranald] & making panegyricks etc yn Desyred'. Outside of the feast, the larger chiefs were supported by a range of retainers, some very functional and others more honorary than actual, such as the person who carried the chief's sword. Some, like Maclean of Duart, also maintained significant numbers of fighting men to help their cause. Descriptions of such men make it clear that on islands like Tiree they were quartered on townships, obtaining their food and clothing from the tenants, but carrying out no farm work in return.

A form of clan display that figured large in clan histories and story-telling was that of feuding. The inter-clan rivalries embodied in the feud were endemic in the Highlands, with some lasting for centuries, such as that between the Frasers and Camerons, a feud that arose over land in Lochaber. Outbreaks of feuding were always greater when strong integrated lordship or control was absent, such as with the eruptions that occurred during the 13th and again, during the sixteenth century. However, some level of feuding was always present in the region prior to the eighteenth century. It formed part of the accepted way by which clans negotiated their relationships. The topographer Martin Martin (1700) said as much when he commented that clan chiefs saw the feud as a form of rivalry played out according to accepted rules. At root, most feuds were triggered by disputes over land possession, the feud being one of the ways in which aggressively-expanding clans could press their case against weaker rivals. The long-running feud between the Campbells of Glenorchy (later Breadalbane) and the Macgregors developed out of a long-running dispute over who occupied land on the border between Argyllshire and Perthshire. Using their position as Crown agents, the Campbells of Glenorchy eventually got the upper hand with the very name Macgregor being proscribed. However, some feuds stemmed from events that reflected on the standing of a clan, such as a failed marriage agreement.

For a chief, appearances were no less vital as a source of display. In a region in which access to metal and to the skills of metalworking was scarce, it was inevitable that chiefs exercised some control over them. Most areas had smiths who worked for the dominant family, such as the James Ofshereden who held Ballishillneach rent-free because he was smith to the Macdonalds of Skye. Special status was accorded to those who produced weaponry and body armour. The production of such armoury was commonly associated with particular families, such as the MacEacherns or Gowans in Morvern or

Rob Roy MacGregor's Grave, Balquhidder

The use of clan names was so powerful in locking individuals into a particular set of loyalties, the Scottish parliament tried to curb what it saw as unruly clans by banning the use of their name. The clan most affected by the proscribing of names was the Clan MacGregor, a clan that had emerged by the fourteenth century. The MacGregors' misfortune was to find themselves in a long-running feud with the Campbells of Glenorchy (later Breadalbane) over the disputed possession or control over farms on the border between Perthshire and Argyllshire. What began as a feud played out on equal terms changed as the Campbells acquired more and more Crown favour. Turning the jurisdiction acquired through this favour against the MacGregors, the latter found themselves outlawed as a clan in 1603 and barred from using the name of MacGregor following a bloody incident in Glenfruin. It is against this background that we need to read the inscription on Rob Roy MacGregor's grave at Balquhidder, 'A Macgregor despite them'. Rob Roy encapsulated the history of the MacGregors, being seen in official sources as 'a notorious robber' and leader of a 'wicked crew of bandits'.

Macfedranes in Benderloch. The importance of such equipment to the personal display behaviour of chiefs and their leading families is shown by the extent to which any sort of commemorative representation of a chief, such as the grave-slabs that were erected in south Argyll during the fifteenth and sixteenth centuries, depict them wearing body armour and holding a claymore.

Chiefly or lordly behaviour derived its power from its exclusiveness. An activity over which they exercised a strong exclusive control was the hunting of game, both animals and fish. As in other parts of Britain, the major landholders reserved areas for hunting. Though these areas were described in charters and place-names as 'Forests', such as the Forest of Harris or Fasnich in Coigach, they

were, in reality, simply areas legally designated for hunting and hawking, often with far more open ground than close or even thin forest cover. The earliest documented examples were to be found in the eastern and southern Highlands, where Anglo-Norman influences first took hold. By the thirteenth century, some, like Strathearn, Atholl and Rothiemurchus, were already established well within the bounds of the Highlands. From the late thirteenth century onwards, documentary references can be found to others further north and west (e.g. Ross, Cluanie, Mamlorne and Lochaber). What we cannot say is whether these designated hunting reserves to the west and north pre-date their first documentary references. The number of deer reported by Dean Munro (1600) as present on islands like Jura together with the presence of hunting forests on Hebridean islands like Harris and Jura suggests that traditional Gaelic chiefs may also have reserved land for hunting and hawking, but we cannot assume that they had the same legal status as those brought into the region with feudalism. However, there can be no doubt that hunting was a

A Chiefly Feast

Feasting may only have been an occasional feature of chiefly life, but, in a world of recurrent scarcity, it was a richly symbolic one. Drawing on the vast quantities of food that many chiefs gathered in as render or as rent, the feast symbolised the chief's capacity to host and to support. Such feasts were held on many occasions, such as to celebrate a marriage alliance or to cement alliances between chiefs and senior kinsmen. A feast would have been the occasion when clan pipers and harpists entertained and when clan historians and genealogists might add the occasion to the store of clan legend.
CHRIS BROWN

favoured pursuit for Gaelic chiefs long before Anglo-Norman influences seeped into the region. Amongst Gaelic chiefs, the preferred method of hunting probably involved a chase, with animals such as deer and boar being chased with greyhounds, mastiffs and other dogs The most commonly reported style in later medieval sources, though, was that of the drive. This used large numbers of men and dogs to drive game towards a group of strategically positioned hunters. Landowners often involved their tenants in their pursuit of hunting and hawking. A seventeenth-century lease issued by the Captain of Clanranald, for instance, bound the tenant to maintain the Captain and his servants 'with hound, haulkis, and their keepers pro rata as the remanent of my country people sall'.

As the practice of early hunting comes into view, we are better able to see the social tensions and conflicts that surrounded hunting reserves. Court records for Rannoch, for instance, show regular instances of tenants or cottagers being charged with the illegal hunting of deer, including one notable instance in 1684 when over 100 deer were killed after being forced out of Rannoch Forest by persistent cold weather. By the seventeenth century, the maintenance of game reserves was in decline. Landowners saw their land as better used for stock production or as a means by which they could provide for the rising number of inhabitants on their estates. As a consequence, we find surviving forests being opened up for settlement by farmers and not just by foresters. Glen Strathfarrar, for instance, was systematically settled from the late sixteenth century onwards, whilst the Forest of Harris acquired small 'bays' of settlement by the late seventeenth century.

An Early Hunting Scene

Driving deer with hounds became the standard form of hunting in the Highlands. A glimpse of how dogs were assembled is provided by a 1632 grant of the lands of Camusnakiest in the Braes of Mar. Each vassal was to give attendance to the Earl of Mar with eight followers from each davoch of land 'with their dogs and hounds, at all his huntings within the bounds of Mar', and they were to build 'lonckartis for the hunting, and sall make and put up further tinchellis [beaters]'.

HISTORIC SCOTLAND

From Townland to Shieling: the Traditional Farming Township

The Challenge of Environment

Just as the ruggedness of the region, its extreme fragmentation into so many self-contained glens and straths, peninsulas and islands, created a challenge for its political integration into the emerging Scottish kingdom over the medieval period, so also did it represent a challenge for the farming communities who relied on its soil for subsistence. Though only a small fraction of the region was physically suitable for cultivation, what stands out about the medieval township is that it valued arable so much. Though most had access to extensive hill or mountain grazings that were used to produce meat, milk, butter and cheese, in practice they gave priority to arable. Indeed, the very definition of townships, the basis on which they were assessed, was their arable core, or what was 'ploughable and bedewable' as one early charter put it, other resources being treated as appendages. Admittedly, arable and pasture were hardly disconnected given the role of the one in providing manure for the other. So dependent was arable on the manure produced by the grazings of the township that Dean Munro referred to arable as 'manurit land' throughout his survey of the Hebrides. The problem for Highland and Hebridean communities, though, was that for all their reliance on arable, the amount of land suitable was tightly prescribed. To maximise what was available, townships had to be opportunistic, squeezing arable into an environment in which cultivable land was sometimes linear, stretched along straths or raised beaches, often patchy and broken, but always limited.

Along the western edge of the Outer Hebrides, many townships lay at the interface between the machair on the seaward side and the peat inland. Indeed, on islands like the Uists, townships positively gained from the mixing of these soils. During expansion, they pushed freely onto peatier soils, using the machair sand to sweeten it and, at greater risk, they pushed out onto the sandier soils, using peat to give the soil more organic content. The problem was that ploughing the sandier soils left them susceptible to erosion because, as a seventeenth-century source on the Uists put it, the 'sand doeth flow with the winds'. Across the medieval period and beyond, many townships in the Hebrides repeatedly faced this problem. The island of Pabbay, for example, lost over 300 acres of its arable on its south-west side to a single storm in the late seventeenth century. A later 1772 report on the island was able to claim that 'the sea flows ... where many people still alive have reaped crops of grain'.

Abandoned House Platforms at Illeray, North Uist

Storms over the seventeenth and eighteenth centuries devastated many areas along the western side of the Long Island and inner Hebridean islands like Coll and Tiree, lifting away the sandier arable soils of some areas and completely overwhelming fields and houses in other areas with sand. Arable fields in the township of Illeray on North Uist were developed on the light sandy soils that fringed the coast. In mid-eighteenth-century storms, large portions of its land were simply blown away, leaving stone trails where dykes once stood and raised house platforms (as seen here) now surrounded by tidal flats.

Framing the Farming Township

The basic unit of landholding around which settlement and farming was organised throughout the Highlands and Islands was the farming township, or toun, known in Gaelic as the *baile*. The most readily available source of evidence for the medieval toun is that of land charters and rentals. These depict the farming toun as defined by an assessment of traditional land units, such as the *davoch* or *pennyland*. Such assessments probably began as renders that were burdened on individuals or families. In time, they were transformed into burdens on land, and thereafter used to measure the amount of arable possessed by a toun and the amount of rent paid by it. We cannot be precise about when this conversion into *land* assessments took place, but it was probably as landholding became feudalised. Along the eastern and southern edges of the Highlands, this is likely to have been during the twelfth century, but it is likely to been much later in the far west.

Once introduced, land assessments formed the basis for leasing out land until the eighteenth century. They defined the amount of arable in a town either by fixing the acreage that could be sown or how much grain could be sown, an approach especially suited to the difficult environments of the far west. Yet even in the more fertile parts of the region, the land covered by the assessment of a toun would have represented only a small proportion of all the land available. The rest would have been pasture or hill ground exploited for pasture, peat and turf on a shared or common basis by those in possession of arable. Land assessments also fixed the amount of rent paid, a rent that could remain unchanged across many generations. When they first come into view, rents comprised a basket of standard food rents, usually grain or meal, poultry and livestock, together with special payments such as fish or plaid, and archaic renders like reeking hens, the latter being a hen paid by every house from which smoke issued. Tenants were also burdened with labour services, from cutting peat to so many days' labour at harvesting. Food rents probably developed out of an earlier obligation that required landholders to maintain their chief or lord and his retinue. A late sixteenth-century report enables us to glimpse the late survival of this obligation in the Hebrides. For a number of islands, the report details the heavy payments of food that were to be provided by tenants for each unit of land assessment as hospitality or support for their chief and his retinue when they came to the island, a right of hospitality known as *cuid-oiche*.

The Runrig Community

Land assessments also affected the landholding character of touns. If we move beyond the tacksmen who leased the land and look at those

A Head-dyke
The head-dyke in the former toun of Greaulin, Skye.

who actually farmed the soil, the majority of touns would appear as farmed by more than one tenant. On the mainland, the farming community tended to be relatively small, with most touns having between two and four tenants, though in those areas where arable was important, the scale of the farm community could be boosted by the presence of crofters, cotters and cottagers attached to the toun. The largest farming communities were those of the Hebrides. Touns on islands such as Tiree and the Uists were physically larger and had much more arable than those on the mainland, so it is hardly surprising that the number of tenants working them was greater, with some having ten or more tenants.

The number of tenants to be found in each town is significant because it formed the basis for the runrig organisation of landholding, where each tenant had his share of the toun scattered in the form of intermixed strips across the toun's arable. In the Hebrides, if not on the mainland or in the Northern Isles, it was common for runrig landholding to be reallocated between landholders on a frequent, even annual, basis. A survey of North Uist in 1799 talked about the estate 'changing the possession yearly'. Such words could be applied to many Hebridean islands in the eighteenth century and before. When we add the runrig fragmentation of landholding, and its regular flux in layout, to the extreme physical fragmentation of arable itself, we can begin to appreciate some of the management complexities posed by the typical runrig toun.

The Highland runrig toun has long been portrayed as an archaic institution whose core features developed during late prehistory and

then survived with little change until the Clearances swept it away. Yet there is actually no concrete evidence to support this. Instead, we should see runrig as belonging to a wider European tradition of open fields. If open fields elsewhere are now seen as having developed fairly late, with the earliest examples appearing in the more fertile regions of western Europe no earlier than the ninth and tenth centuries AD, and spreading outwards over the next three or four centuries, then we have no reason for seeing runrig as having its own chronology, one that would separate it out from this wider European context. Indeed, runrig was probably amongst the last types of open field to develop in Europe. Its appearance in the Highlands was probably linked to the late spread of feudal ideas on landholding and the imposition of land assessments from the twelfth century onwards. The spread of runrig and the assessment of touns were linked because each unit of land assessment denoted a proportionate number of shares in the toun. As a term, runrig was used to describe the dividing out of these shares into holdings on the ground. This division took place frequently because the typical Highland peasant held his land on a year-to-year basis.

Township Resources

The traditional farming toun exploited a range of different resources. At its core, and determining the township's focus or location, was its arable. Always the lower, more sheltered land, the most striking

Summer Grazing

All farming touns faced the need to remove stock from around arable during the growing season. In most Highland and Hebridean touns, this was when stock were taken to the more remote grazings available, usually the shielings. Often, these were quite extensive grazings but could be located as much as 5 or 6 miles away and shared with other nearby townships, each having an assigned area of graze for its stock. The time spent at the shielings was used for making cheese and butter. In a countryside that still had wolves down to the early eighteenth century, grazing stock on the open hills required close shepherding.
CHRIS BROWN

feature about arable in many Highland touns was its broken and uneven character. Only a few areas possessed ground conditions that enabled them to lay out arable as a continuous block of cultivated land, and even fewer had the kind of regular field structure that we associate with the modern landscape. In the majority of touns, arable was an irregular, discontinuous area interspersed with patches of grass, stone outcrops or waterlogged ground. The cultivated land was invariably surrounded by a dyke, usually of stone or turf and stone. In the Outer Hebrides, this dyke would have been a simple affair, stretching round the entire arable. In the Inner Hebrides and across the mainland though, many touns had two dykes, an inner dyke surrounding the core of their arable or infield, meadow land and wintering ground and an outer dyke, called the head dyke, that surrounded both their infield and a more extensively cropped area known as outfield that was usually more grass than arable. Beyond the head dyke, lay the hill pasture. For many touns, their hill pasture could be a varied and extensive area. Parts might be grazed exclusively by stock of a single toun, with each farmer having his stock proportioned or *soumed* according to the amount of land that he held within the toun. Other grazings might be shared with stock from other touns. Where summer pastures were set at distance, touns exploited them via shielings, or temporary summer sites.

Each of these different sectors played a role within the toun economy that was linked to a calendar of routines. These routines were usually enforced through acts passed by the local township or barony court. For touns across the mainland and parts of the Inner Hebrides, the key to their exploitation was the need to maintain the fertility of their core arable or infield, a sector that was maintained in continuous cultivation for oats and bere. In most cases, this fertility was maintained by applications of stock manure. After harvest, stock grazed the harvest stubble, manuring the ground in the process. Over winter, the toun's winterings, which included the grass interspersed with arable, provided the sheltered pasture needed to maintain stock. At night, cattle, horses and even sheep were housed in byres, with the manure accumulated over winter being added to the infield arable in spring.

The outfield was an area of more extensive cultivation than infield. It was cropped on a piecemeal basis with between a quarter and a half being put under crop each year. After each part was cropped for two or three years with oats, it was left to grass over again for a few years before being brought under crop again. Outfield arable was manured by the nightly *tathing*, or folding, of stock during summer on that part due to be cultivated the following summer. Though sometimes seen as a cropping system of great antiquity because of its similarity to shifting cultivation, the creation of outfield probably dated from when the growth of touns pushed the expansion of arable beyond infield. In some cases, this could well have been during the population growth of the twelfth and thirteenth centuries but there are good reasons for believing that in parts of the Highlands, it may not have been until as late as the sixteenth and seventeenth centuries.

Touns in the Outer Hebrides followed a different strategy to that based on infield-outfield. On most islands, cropping was based on a grass–arable system, effectively an outfield system that embraced all their arable. The adoption of such a system may have been encouraged by how arable was calculated, with touns being allocated so many bolls of sowing. On Tiree, each davoch of land, the standard assessment for a toun on the island, was permitted to sow 48 bolls of oats and 24 bolls of bere or barley. As a system, this was more flexible when faced with ground broken by thin soils, rock outcrops or waterlogging, but, this said, Tiree actually possessed far more continuous arable than most parts of the Highlands and Islands. A contributory factor may have been the use of seaweed rather than animal dung as manure. Seaweed released touns from the need to distinguish between arable that depended on winter manure and that which depended on summer manure.

In most touns, stock had to be moved beyond the head dyke once the growing season was under way, usually 1 May, and to be taken to the summer pastures or shielings by 15 June. Occupied for little more than 8–10 weeks at the height of summer, many shieling sites comprised temporary or short-lived structures, including bivouacs or turf dwellings. In the calendar, this was a time when women and children were engaged in making cheese and butter. The hill pastures had uses other than for pasture. Touns freely used them to cut peat for

Peat Cutting
The cutting of peat was usually regulated by local courts, with tenants having to work with the face of the cutting and to restore the turf afterwards.

both fuel and for manure. Like so much activity, peat-cutting was closely regulated, with by-laws requiring those cutting peat to close up the hags behind them. Hill ground also provided a range of other resources, such as heather and ferns. Heather had varied uses, from thatch to dye. Ferns were used as thatch, bedding and manure. Many touns also cut turf from their hill or non-arable ground for use as manure, fuel, for the construction of turf or stone and turf dykes, house walls and as a foundation for roof thatch. After use in this way, turf was generally composted along with the thatch and added to arable as a manure.

A particularly important resource but one already in short supply in many parts of the Highlands and Islands by the medieval period was timber. Its prime use was for building, wattle, bark and even leaf fodder rather than fuel. Relatively large timbers were needed for roof couples, and smaller pieces for doors, room partitions, ploughs, spade and for the handles of crooked spades known as cas-chroms, whilst wattle-based houses and fences could consume vast quantities of saplings, particularly hazel. But even where timber was locally plentiful, landowners exercised strict control over what could be harvested, and over what tenants paid for basics like roof couples, plough stilts and spade handles. More frequently, though, such regulations come to light more in the breach than the observance, with long-run court records, such as those for Menzies and Rannoch in Perthshire, being full of instances in which tenants were charged with stealing oak and hazel. Even in Knoydart, the most isolated inhabited area on the western seaboard, its early eighteenth-century court records contain references to tenants being fined for stealing timber, especially 'watling', a form of timber much in use for the houses of the area. Elsewhere, we can measure the value placed on timber by the way farmers leaving the tenancy of a farm were allowed to take roof couples and doors with them, a custom exercised everywhere from the Hebrides to the Grampians.

Symbolic Landscapes

For the traditional Highland or Hebridean farming community, the various parts of the toun would, at one level, have fitted into a structured cycle of resource use, one that matched various types of need with the changing opportunities offered by the different seasons. At another level, though, their understanding of why and how crops grew and stock reproduced themselves, of what maintained the overall fertility of the land, would have been part of a symbolic landscape. This symbolic landscape linked fertility to a particular way of doing things. There were good reasons why folk concepts of fertility survived alongside organised religion. Traditional society did not understand the real basis of plant growth or sources of fertility, though they understood the need for additives like manure. In a world in which margins were drawn so tightly as to threaten survival whenever sharp fluxes in output occurred, we cannot be surprised that farming communities clung to folk beliefs thought to have a role in ensuring their survival.

The sort of mental landscape that existed can be illustrated by traces of a fire cult that appear most legibly in the eastern Highlands. It involved an annual ritual whereby a bonfire was lit on a prominent hill then used to light a series of torches. These torches were taken by farmers and their families down to their farms then walked, sunwise, around a field, the farmstead and the byre, before being used to relight the farmstead's fire. What might be an associated piece of symbolism can be seen in Strathavon, an area where kirk session records show fire cults to have been well-established. Fields in a number of Strathavon touns had a field, usually the most fertile, named *The Lost*. Literally translated, the name means a kneading trough. Another possibility though is that the word is based on *losaid*, meaning a fire, and refers to the field around which the farmers and their families annually processed with the ritual torch in order to symbolically fertilise the fields.

Another ritual that was full of symbolism was the use of sun-division to divide land. There were various reasons why land needed to be divided, from the inheritance of estates between co-heirs to the dividing out of shares between tenants in a runrig toun. Sun-division provided a basis for this. By it, shares in a toun were differentiated into sunny and shadow shares. If a landholder had the former, he was given the strips to the east or south in each sequence of runrig allocation, whilst if given the shadow portion, he had the strips that lay to the west or north. However, sun-division also involved an ordering of movement, as well as allocation. Early Scottish legal texts make it clear that the allocation of land began at dawn to the east, and worked its way sunwise around the toun. A feature of sun-division is that when used to differentiate shares, landholders could use not only the terms sunny/shadow, but also, terms like east/west, upper/nether and *mor/beag*. These descriptions were not only seen as equivalent, but also as interchangeable. A sequence of late seventeenth-century rentals for touns in Trotternish (Skye), for instance, lists the twin touns of Trumpan Mor and Trumpan Beg, the divided halves of a single davoch. However, in one rental, they appear as Trumpan East and West, as if the local community still used *mor/beag* and east/west interchangeably.

The Toun Economy

The amount of arable in the Highlands and Islands was only around 9 per cent of the total land surface available even at its peak in the early

Change and the Early Farming Toun

Far from being a settlement form that survived the centuries without change, the Highland farming toun needs to be seen as an institution that experienced change. This diagram tries to summarise some of the long-term changes and adjustments that affected touns on the mainland, including the possible flux between dispersed and nucleated settlement; the splitting of touns as units of landholding into east/west, *mor/beag* portions; the building of an inner dyke around infield or the land originally defined by the land assessments of a toun; the creation of areas of outfield cropping surrounded by a new outer dyke; the growth of outsets around the edge of established touns; and the upgrading of temporary shieling sites into permanent settlements.

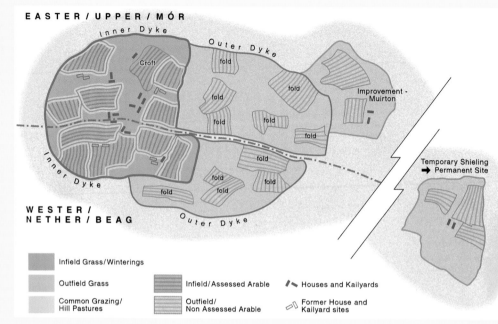

EASTER / UPPER / MÓR

Inner Dyke

Outer Dyke

Croft

fold

fold

fold

Improvement - Muirton

fold

fold

fold

Inner Dyke

fold

fold

fold

fold

fold

fold

WESTER / NETHER / BEAG

Outer Dyke

Temporary Shieling → Permanent Site

	Infield Grass/Winterings
	Outfield Grass
	Common Grazing/Hill Pastures
	Infield/Assessed Arable
	Outfield/Non Assessed Arable
	Houses and Kailyards
	Former House and Kailyard sites

nineteenth century. A similar proportion may have been cultivated during the climatic optimum of the twelfth and thirteenth centuries, when population may have been at an equal high. Yet despite its limited availability, arable was at the heart of the traditional township economy. It provided the bulk of people's diet and formed the cornerstone for the payment of rents in kind. The key field crops grown were oats and bere. Oats was the dietary staple for most communities. Bere was used for beer and, later, whisky, though areas capable of producing large amounts of bere, such as Tiree and the Uists, also used it for making barley bread. Despite their modest arable acreages and low margins in terms of the returns on seed, Highland and Hebridean touns also handed over a considerable surplus of grain as rent. Isolation or environmental hardship were no disqualification to being levied with rents based on oatmeal or bere. Even islands like Ensay and Pabbay, two islands that lay between Harris and North Uist, were burdened with substantial payments of grain as rent, as was St Kilda!

West Highland Township
Reconstruction of a West Highland township on the eve of the Clearances.
CHRIS BROWN

Though grass and stock played a major role within the economy of townships, meat had only a modest place in the traditional Highland diet. From a dietary point of view, stock were more valued as a source of milk, butter and cheese. All touns produced milk, butter and cheese, with hints in some sources that certain touns may have specialised in producing cheese. Of course, beyond their dietary role, stock were also important for a range of stock products, all of which had fundamental uses within the traditional toun: wool, hides or leather, bone, horn and tallow. For some coastal touns, fish would have provided a supplementary source of food, though much depended on circumstance. Despite the widely held view that fish were never as important for the Hebridean as they were for communities in the Northern Isles, tenants and cottagers in many coastal touns would have made the effort to catch some fish as a dietary supplement if only on a small scale and if only by fishing inshore waters. Where significant quantities of fish are recorded in early rentals, they tended to be from a few specialised holdings that handed over part of their catch as rent. Kilbride on Loch Fyne, for example, paid over half of its herring catch as rent.

Easter Bleaton township

The remains of a pre-clearance township at Easter Bleaton, Glenshee, Perthshire
RCAHMS

The Shape of Highland Settlement

The traditional Highland toun is usually seen as worked from a single nucleated settlement made up of an amorphous cluster of dwellings, byres, buildings for storing peat, kilns for drying grain, kailyards and enclosures for penning stock. When we look at the pre-crofting or pre-Clearance settlement depicted in eighteenth- or nineteenth-century estate plans, we find many touns whose settlement fits this stereotype of a single nucleated cluster of buildings. However, there were exceptions. Some, especially those to be found along the Glens to the east and south-east of the region, are best described as linear rather than nuclear in layout, their dwellings and outbuildings strewn in a thin straggling line between the arable on the lower slopes and the hill pastures above. A fine example of this sort of toun can be seen at Easter Bleaton in Glenshee. Equally interesting are those touns whose settlement lay in scattered groups or clusters rather than bundled together on a single site. A fine example of this sort is provided by Rosal in Strathnaver, a toun mapped by the Sutherland estate in 1807. We can identify a number of settlement *foci* on the 1807 plan, each a separate cluster of buildings and kailyards. Field survey has confirmed this pattern, locating the wall-footings of former dwellings and outbuildings at four separate sites.

Though we can draw on the results of a number of large-scale excavations, we are not yet in a position to say conclusively how such settlements evolved over the medieval period. Some have argued that, as with villages and townships elsewhere in western Europe, the nucleated settlement of the Highland toun, as well as the landholding structure of the toun itself, may not have emerged until the spread of feudal ideas on landholding and the imposition of land assessments. In the Highlands, this is unlikely to have taken placed until at least the twelfth–fourteenth centuries. The imposition of large blocks of land assessment over landholding may have been significant in encouraging the nucleation of settlement, because it meant farmers became attached to particular blocks of land assessment and were forced to join together in the work routines that were required to exploit its arable and to have a shared responsibility for its rent. Prior to this point, settlement and landholding may have been organised around a more dispersed pattern of settlement, comprising individual farmsteads or small clusters. Those touns that still had more dispersed patterns of settlement down into the eighteenth century may preserve elements of this earlier pattern. Where attempts have been made to excavate such settlements, some have been shown to be early features. At Druim nan Dearcag, beside Loch Olabhat on North Uist, for instance, a small cluster of domestic and non-domestic buildings within the bounds of the toun of Foshigarry, but at some distance from the main settlement focus, were dated to the late medieval or immediate post-medieval period.

Others, however, have proposed a different interpretation for how settlement developed. Large-scale surveys carried out across a range of touns on South Uist have pointed to continuity between, on the one hand, late prehistoric and Viking settlement and, on the other, the eighteenth-century toun. The fact that most eighteenth-century touns appeared to have Iron Age, Pictish and Viking settlement within their bounds suggested that the broad layout of eighteenth-century touns may have been based on a pattern of landholding that had taken shape by the late Iron Age and which survived, through later Viking settlement and beyond. Excavation at a number of these sites (eg Milton) has also led to the suggestion that there may also have been a continuous occupation of the same areas of settlement from the Iron Age down to the eighteenth century. However, this was settlement continuity only in a generalised sense. It did not lead to the sort of large settlement mound that we see at The Udal, on the northern tip of North Uist, where complex layers of occupation have accumulated directly over each other from prehistory down to the early modern period. Indeed, eighteenth-century settlement in these South Uist touns was often at a distance (e.g. 200–300 metres) from the Iron Age, Pictish and Viking sites, whilst on Machair Mheadhanach, shifts in settlement layout were detected, dated to *circa* thirteenth century.

The Blackhouse, Arnol
The blackhouse, Number 42, at Arnol is now preserved. Its interior shows that part used as a byre, in which cattle and horses would have been housed over night during winter.
The manure so accumulated would have been spread on the arable in spring (mainly the bere crop, but, later, the potato crop) along with the soot-enriched thatch (see photograph below).
NATIONAL MUSEUMS OF SCOTLAND
(Above)

Medieval settlement was not simply about whether settlement became more nucleated or not at some point during the Middle Ages. The widespread splitting of touns in response to family settlements, sales, or simply the problems of growth, introduced an opposite trend. As a factor, such disaggregation was particularly influential in the eastern Highlands and may be a factor in explaining why touns in the east of region were smaller in size than touns in the far west. Gordon of Straloch, an early topographer, actually referred to the extensive splitting of touns in Strathbogie during the late sixteenth century as a reorganisation intended to make touns smaller. It could produce complex on-the-ground arrangements. A toun and its settlement could undergo a split into east and west halves, then one half could be split into upper and nether halves and then, to compound matters still further, one of these halves (or a quarter of the original toun) could be divided, runrig-like, into sunny and shadow halves. In these same areas, the late medieval period also saw a different form of disaggregation, as old-established touns acquired a periphery of small, satellite settlements with names that belied their origin, such as Newtoun, Muirtoun or Bogtoun. Beyond areas of established settlement, the early modern period also saw a wave of settlement creation based on the conversion of temporary shielings into permanently occupied touns, as with Lettermore and Blairnamorrow in Strathavon (see diagram on page 34).

These shifts in settlement layout were assisted by the nature of peasant housing. There is still a great deal to be learned about peasant housing during the medieval period, about how it changed and the nature of its regional variants. Though some traditional Hebridean housing, like the blackhouse of the Outer Hebrides, may have an appearance of great antiquity, the examples that have survived into modern times are of nineteenth-century origin. A study of North Uist compared what appeared on a detailed early nineteenth-century estate plan with what still existed in the landscape during the mid-twentieth century and concluded that nothing surviving in the modern landscape dated back to beyond the early nineteenth century. In fact, subsequent excavations at The Udal on North Uist concluded that, as a building style, the black house could not be traced back via an unbroken lineage to Norse dwellings in the area, despite their similarity in style.

Generally, pre-eighteenth-century peasant housing was smaller in size when compared to that being built by the eighteenth century. Most also had more rounded corners, to the extent of being more oval than rectangular in plan. The dwellings excavated at Druim nan Dearcag, on North Uist, for instance, were oval in shape, their internal floor space measuring 4 metres by 2 metres. Dwellings that incorporated space for stock under the same roof, so-called longhouses or byre-houses, were invariably greater in length. Some of the Viking examples recently excavated on South Uist measured 8 metres by 4 metres, and had rounded corners and slightly bowed walls. A form of medieval longhouse found on the higher ground of north-east Perthshire and called a Pitcarmick-type dwelling had a more elongated oval shape, often with curving walls and sometimes with a small enclosure attached to them. In length, most were between 10 and 25 metres, being clearly larger than those found in the west of the region.

Prior to the mid-eighteenth century, we also find more extensive use being made of perishable materials like turf for house and byre walls, either as part of a turf and dry-stone mix, as a wall capping, as a base for roof thatch, or for the entire wall itself. By its very nature, such housing had a temporary character. Thatch was removed and composted annually, whilst the turf from the roof base and from house walls was also recycled as manure, albeit after a few years of use. When we set this reuse of turf alongside the practice whereby tenants were allowed to remove roof timbers and doors at the end of their tenure and alongside the fact that many Highland tenants held land on a year-to-year basis, we can begin to appreciate how ephemeral some peasant housing must have been. Settlement would have been in a constant state of flux, as thatch, roof timbers and turf were regularly removed and replaced. Those areas that used wattle or creel for house walls, such as Lochaber, were equally affected by the need for frequent renewal. With dwellings shifting in and out of use, it is easy to see how settlement layout might adjust easily to the changes that took place in the landholding context of settlement. Where turf and creel houses once stood in such settlements might now be traceable only through subtle variations in soil chemistry.

A Peat House
Huts built of peat or turf were once common in the Highlands and Islands. A Department of Health report drawn up just after World War I even reported a number recently constructed wholly of peat on North Uist. Their measurements suggest they compared closely in size with the example shown in the photograph. Back in the 1770s, Dr Samuel Johnson and James Boswell stayed in a three-roomed inn at Anoch at Glen Morriston that was built entirely of turf, from its walls to its roof, all designed and pieced together by the landlord.
NATIONAL MUSEUMS OF SCOTLAND

Township at The Udal
Remains of the township at The Udal, North Uist, abandoned in the 1690s.

The Highlands Beyond Farming

A World of Little Commonwealths

In an effort to portray the sort of world that existed before markets led to the specialisation of labour, the famous Scottish economist Adam Smith pointed to the Highlands and Islands and to how each farmer could be his own ploughmaker, smith, weaver, shoemaker, carpenter and baker. For much of the medieval period, there must have been many touns in which his portrayal would have rung true. When it came to basic needs, from the making of farm tools to house construction, from the weaving or dyeing of cloth to the tanning of leather, most households would have been self-sufficient, families and communities drawing on a wide range of techniques and resources to satisfy their own needs and creating in the process what some described as 'little commonwealths'. Some resources were improvised for a particular purpose, such as grass for rope or bone for utensils. Other scarce resources, like timber or iron, were endlessly recycled until they were simply worn out.

Of course, not everyone acted as his own weaver or wright, or was architect of his own dwelling. Surrounding the wealthier members of society were a number of specialised craftsmen or tradesmen. In the medieval period, some of these more specialised crafts or trades were concentrated in families, even to the extent of forming distinct kin groups or mini-clans. This was especially the case with those status crafts or trades that serviced large and powerful chiefdoms. The Beatons, for instance, were hereditary doctors for the Lordship of the Isles, skilled in the use of leeches, herbals and other remedies. The Gowans were armourers, a craft that would have been tightly controlled by chiefs given the relative scarcity of iron and the military value of items like the claymore and light body armour.

In some cases, the hereditary status of such crafts was reinforced by the reward of holdings set on favourable terms to them, so they ranked as farmers as much as craftsmen. In some cases, where roles were mundane, holdings might have been small. For those whose craft gave them status, more substantial holdings were involved. A 1718 rental, for instance, Smisary in Moidart, a mainland toun more easily reached by sea until the mid-twentieth century, was held by Donald McGillichallam, 'Boatwright or Carpenter to Clanranald'. A craft dependent on the wealthier more powerful members of society was that of stonemasonry. Most of those who helped build the numerous castles and tower houses that mushroomed during the twelfth–fifteenth centuries probably belonged to itinerant groups of stonemasons, working where their commissions took them. By comparison, the distinctive monumental gravestones that were erected in different parts of Argyll during the late fifteenth and sixteenth centuries were more likely to have been carved by a school of stonemasons who resided locally. The way in which they depicted local chiefs and landowners, or senior members of their family, with all the perceived trappings of status, makes it clear that this was a tradition of stonemasonry that depended on a status-conscious society.

Milling the Corn

Despite Adam Smith's observations, landowners did not expect the ordinary farming community to be entirely self-sufficient in all crafts or trades. In areas that produced significant grain surpluses, landowners built large vertical mills (based on the waterwheel) attached to a mill croft. Most parishes sited around the southern or eastern edges of the Highlands boasted such a mill. Tenants in the surrounding touns were then forced by their tacks to have all their corn ground there by an obligation known as *thirling*. The miller abstracted a payment or *multure* from the grain processed by him, and the landowner, in turn, was able to charge the miller a rent that far exceeded the value of the croft itself. Wherever they operated, millers had a difficult relationship with local tenants. On the Cromartie estate, eighteenth-century tenants complained bitterly about the miller at Knockarthur, Robert McKay. He was a wright by trade and was said to have 'no Skill or notion of the Mill, or of manageing the miln only greed Enough to take up the Multur Extravagantly'. Such feeling undoubtedly captured some of the tensions that lay just beneath the surface in many other touns.

Further into the main body of the Highlands, or to the west, the presence of mills thinned greatly. The mill in Knapdale was seen as so exceptional that it was regarded as one of the wonders of Knapdale. Even large islands like Arran only had four conventional mills, so that many of its 90 or so touns were sited some distance away from the nearest mill. Tiree, easily one of the most productive in the Hebrides, had only three vertical mills, including a windmill. By the middle decades of the eighteenth century, one of the vertical mills was reported as suffering repeated problems of water supply and the windmill at Scarinish was in need of repair. South Uist suffered similar problems, with both its vertical mills at Howmore and Boisdale routinely suffering from water supply problems. Sporadic water flow was a problem for milling everywhere, but more so where large vertical mills were located at the edge of their operational range. Such problems were made worse if such mills did not have access to sufficient local grain and had to draw grain from an extensive catchment and, often, over difficult terrain. Not surprisingly, farmers

A Horizontal Mill, Lewis
Early horizontal or ladle mill at Arnol, Lewis.
NATIONAL MUSEUMS OF SCOTLAND

A Hand Quern
Woman using a hand quern.
NATIONAL MUSEUMS OF SCOTLAND

thirled to them preferred simpler, more local solutions, especially if inadequate water made the mill's operations uncertain.

As an alternative, some touns had access to a small horizontal or ladle mill that could service a single toun. However, the most widespread solution where touns produced only small amounts of grain, or were set at a distance from a mill, was to use the hand quern. Like many solutions in the region, it called for heavy investments of labour. Travellers like Thomas Pennant were struck by the sheer number of women who were employed for months on end grinding grain with the quern. When estates began to order the destruction of querns, a move first made on Tiree as early as the 1730s, it was prompted as much by the concern to free up this labour for other tasks, such as spinning or knitting, as by a desire to force tenants into using vertical mills.

Clothing the Highlander

Clothmaking was one of the most basic and enduring crafts for any traditional society. Prior to the eighteenth century, most farm households would have made all their own cloth and the clothes based on them, whether woven or knitted. Basic tasks like spinning, weaving, dyeing and fulling were part of the annual routines of life, filling the gaps in the farming calendar. The extent of cloth production is well conveyed by the earliest available rentals. Early rental lists for touns in areas like Strathavon, as well as for touns on islands like Tiree, Lewis and Lismore, show cloth being routinely collected in as rent. In the case of the tenants of Iona abbey, the cloth was 'white, black and grey', but in many instances elsewhere, it was listed simply as plaid. The widespread nature of its production would certainly account for the variety of plaid, with communities across the region drawing on local techniques of weave, dyes and the like. Linen, too, was produced widely, using locally grown flax, and, in some cases, such as on Lismore, it was paid as rent. There is no basis for assuming that ordinary farmers marketed cloth, though the temptation to do so when they lived close to markets like Inverness must have been high. However, the scale of cloth gathered in by estates like the Lewis estate or, in the east, the Gordon estate, suggests estates must have had a marketable surplus beyond their own domestic needs.

By the eighteenth century, more organised efforts were being made to develop cloth production. Attracted by the presence of cheap

Woman Knitting, near Stornoway, Lewis

In a letter amongst the Sutherland Estate Papers, there is a note entitled 'Mr Keith's Scheme for Sutherland'. It argues for the introduction of knitting manufacture as a solution for the region and its perceived underemployment of labour. It was not as difficult to learn as lint spinning, he wrote, and could be practised by everyone, male and female, adult and children, from 7 to 70 years old, 'even while drawing their peats, or manuring their land, and they can work at it sitting, standing or [as in the photograph above] walking'.

NATIONAL MUSEUMS OF SCOTLAND

Spinning, Lewis

Woman spinning outside a blackhouse, Lewis. This sort of scene would have been commonplace back in the eighteenth century and before.

NATIONAL MUSEUMS OF SCOTLAND

labour, and the domestic traditions of the industry, dealers began to draw key domestic processes like spinning and weaving into a production chain that took it far beyond the household economy. They provided wool and flax for spinning and yarn for weaving, particularly to families around the southern and eastern edges of the Highlands. In some areas, those attempting to take control of the industry were small dealers or merchants operating through key towns like Inverness or fairs like Muthil in Perthshire. Following Culloden, the British Linen Bank attempted to establish the foundation of a large-scale domestic linen industry. Responding to what it saw as the idleness of the poorer tenants and cottagers, it built up an extensive network of several thousand spinners and weavers across areas like Cromarty, Badenoch, Strathspey, and Strathavon. Working out of towns like Inverness, Tain, Cromarty and Dingwall, agents of the bank provided the capital for the initial purchase of spindles and looms, then kept those involved supplied with hemp, flax or yarn. Supplementing their efforts were those of the Board of Trustees, the body charged with running the estates forfeited after the Jacobite Rebellion of 1745, who built spinning and heckling stations in Glen Morriston and at Lochs Broom and Carron. Despite their efforts though, the sheer distances involved in the production chain proved the industry's undoing. By the 1770s, the British Linen Bank had ceased to trade and though some linen production continued on a smaller scale, the industry never realised its early expectations.

Highland Dress

The typical dress of the West Highland woman prior to the mid-eighteenth century consisted of the kerchief and the tonnac, or short plaid. The men wore bonnets, short coats, philabegs, tartan short hose and, when needed, plaiding wrapped around the body and shoulders. Writing in 1727, George Wade, the army officer responsible for building new roads in the region in the aftermath of the 1715 uprising, reported that it was 'seen to be a reproach to a Highlander to be seen without his Musket, Broad Sword, Pistol and Dirk. These by a long Custom were esteem'd part of their Dress … worn by the Meanest of the Inhabitants, even in their Churches, Fairs and Markets'. After the '45, the government banned the carrying of weapons and the wearing of Highland dress by an act of 1747. The parish reports in the *Old Statistical Account* that were published in the 1790s, after the ban on Highland dress had been lifted, suggest that it had a visible and long-term effect in most areas. Furthermore, when the wearing of tartan recovered, it tended to be based on the cloth produced by the larger manufactories and to be more standardised in its representation of particular tartan setts than those produced locally or domestically before the '45.

Brewing and Distilling

Brewing had a long history in the Highlands, but whisky or *aquavitae* was probably not distilled in the region until around the sixteenth century. As with any other trade that offered potential profit, or was capable of creating disorder, brewing and distilling were closely regulated by landowners and the authorities, but these regulations were flouted with equal dedication in the more isolated touns. Just as rentals refer to mill-crofts, so also do we find references to all the trappings of the drinks trade: brewseats, maltkilns, and changehouses.

Changehouses were the places at which ale and spirits were sold, but many also functioned as the holdings or cottages at which ale was brewed and whisky distilled. On the larger estates, brewseats, kilns and changehouses were leased like any other holdings. Skeabost on Skye, for example, was leased to the tenant in 1754 with the privilege of 'brewing, malting, vending and Distilling all sorts of legal Spirits and liquors therein'. Like all such trades, brewers and distillers were constantly at odds with those who used them. The malt kiln at Killin, for instance, was said to ill serve local farmers, its malt making 'sober malt' except what the brewer supplied for his own needs and 'to his favourites'. From the very outset, whisky distilling was both probably split between official stills, regulated by estates and processing bere from a wide area, and small illicit stills tucked away into the more inaccessible corners of touns and processing bere from a single holding or toun. Occasionally, we can glimpse the scale of this illicit distilling. On Tiree, for example, a survey of 1730 reported over 50 stills on the island, more than one for each toun. A survey of Coigach Barony on the mainland opposite Skye reported 'No Maltsters, Brewers or Distillers', but, given that the same report could say 'Whiskie is Retail'd in ten or twelve Hutts', we can conclude that illicit distilling was clearly widespread. Initially, however, this question of who was licensed and who was not may have been confused. Across the eastern Grampians, it was possible to find local districts in which each toun was burdened with small payments of whisky (eg a pint or quart) as part of its rent. Whether these touns were distilling it themselves or whether they commissioned 'official' distillers to produce on their behalf is not clear. On Colonsay, virtually every toun was burdened with payments of whisky, yet no public maltkiln or distiller existed on the island.

Whisky Distilling

As the authorities and estates tried to regulate whisky distilling over the eighteenth century, illicit distilling moved to the remoter niches of the more isolated touns. As this reconstruction shows, the needs of distilling were simple, though the turf used as fuel was an increasing problem.
CHRIS BROWN

Concerned as much with the loss of revenue to themselves as with its social order implications, and concerned with what they saw as a misuse of scarce subsistence, both landowners and government began to regulate distilling more strictly by the mid-eighteenth century. Estates like the Argyll estate made efforts to stamp out illicit distilling. In a sense, though, they had helped to create the problem in the first place by replacing payments of bere with cash payments during the seventeenth century. Tenants found themselves with large bere surpluses and a demand for cash rents. Not surprisingly, some turned to illicit distilling as a source of this cash, so by the time the Earl of Argyll demanded that illicit distilling be suppressed on his estate, it had become an essential part of the household economy, the means by which many smaller tenants raised the cash needed for the earl's rent. Yet there were estates that saw the suppression of illicit distilling as an opportunity to expand its own interests. On Jura, for instance, some touns acquired special storehouses built for making malt, whilst others were required to deliver so much of their bere crop to them. With stills on the islands and many more around nearby Campbelton, the south Argyll area was a major area of production. Indeed, by the 1790s, the stills of the Campbelton area alone were said to consume half the 20,000 bolls of bere being turned into whisky in Argyll. By this point, high levels of duty and tighter regulation by customs officers was stamping out illicit distilling everywhere, so that output was increasingly concentrated into fewer but more regulated stills. The decline of the illicit still over the closing decades of the eighteenth century, though, brought the larger regulated stills into greater prominence, including some that were to be amongst the most famous of whiskies, such as Bowmore and Lagavulin on Islay.

The Harvest of the Seas

As pressure on land rose over the eighteenth century, the need to maximise alternative sources of subsistence also increased. Fishing, at least for those living along the western seaboard or in the Hebrides, acquired a new importance. Most official commentaries on the region saw fishing as underexploited, but what they had in mind was the large-scale commercial exploitation of fishing. If we look at late eighteenth-century descriptions, every toun along the coast was said to have one or two boats and fishing gear which it used to fish in the bays, sea lochs and inshore waters around it. Wherever we find detailed comment on such coastal touns, most used fishing as a supplement. Most tenants in Knoydart, for instance, joined with Clydesiders in fishing for herring in Loch Nevis, whilst fish were said

Lagavulin distillery
A nineteenth-century engraving of the distillery at Lagavulin, Islay.

Ullapool
Ordnance Survey Map of Ullapool, a British Fisheries village planned out in 1788.
NATIONAL LIBRARY OF SCOTLAND

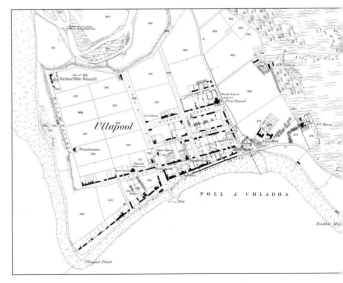

to be found around Gigha in 'such Quantities that they [the tenants] catch them in blankets'. Needless to say, in years when harvests were poor, or as holding size per family fell over the eighteenth century, we can expect farmers everywhere to have resorted to fishing more often.

By the closing decades of the eighteenth century, some communities became heavily committed to fishing, so that they are better described as fishing communities who also had access to a small amount of arable rather than vice versa. In Assynt, for instance, touns on the coast, such as Baddidarroch and Culack, accumulated large numbers of sub-tenants, who were forced, by virtue of having barely an acre or so per family, to rely heavily on fishing for subsistence and rent. As fishing settlements, these Assynt touns were encouraged by the Sutherland estate, their tacksmen being required by their leases to sublet the land to those engaged in fishing.

Other estates were pursuing similar policies by the second half of the eighteenth century, following the example of the British Fisheries Society in laying out settlements based on fisher-crofts. The British Fisheries Society developed a number of fishing villages in the region, like Ullapool and Tobermory. Its approach was to provide the infrastructure. At Ullapool, it laid out a series of fisher-crofts in 1788, each with boats, nets, sheds and an arable plot of a size that meant extra sources of diet or income were still needed. Two types of fishermen lived in such settlements. First, there were those who simply used the settlement as a base for inshore fishing, often smaller tenants sharing a boat. Second, there were those who became involved in a more commercial scale of fishing, using larger vessels funded by Highland proprietors or Lowland companies. The cod fishery based at Gairloch, for instance, was funded by Sir Hector Mackenzie of Gairloch. Five or six fishing boats, known as busses, worked out of Ullapool itself by the 1790s, their fish cured and barrelled at a herring house built within the town. More herring busses worked from the fishing stations established some years later on both Isle Martin and Isle

Tanera. The fish were sent both to Clydeside and Liverpool, the latter being used as a source of salt for the industry.

Highland Woods and Forests: Mythical and Otherwise

Even by the time of Somerled, wood was a scarce resource in parts of the Highlands and Islands. This was certainly true of the Hebrides. Though woodland is now thought to have been present in the Hebrides during the post-glacial period, much had retreated or had been cleared by the end of the prehistoric period. Even during the Viking period, most Hebridean communities would have struggled to satisfy basic timber needs and would have depended on supplies from the Scottish mainland or, for large timbers, from Norway. When we look at the region during the early modern period, few touns had local access to woodland, except on islands like Islay and Mull.

Oak-birch Woods, Glenelg
Part of the MacLeod of MacLeod estate until the late eighteenth century, these oak–birch woods at Glenelg were used by tenants from Harris, Skye and Glenelg for the timber needed for wattle, roof couples, ploughs and cas-chroms.

Fishing
Fishing off the west coast, especially for herring, was a group activity as both locals and foreigners tracked the concentrated movement of shoals. 'From that time [September]', reported one source, 'their appearance, though exceedingly irregular, is anxiously looked for, till the month of February. Great is the preparation made, and much the expense incurred ... the people are instantly afloat, with every species of seaworthy craft - numerous crews from all parts of the east and west coasts of Scotland, and even from Ireland, press forward with the utmost eagerness to the field of slaughter - sloops, schooners, wherries, boats of all sizes, are seen constantly flying on the wings of the wind, from creek to creek, and from loch to loch, according as the varying reports of men, or the noisy flight of birds, or tumbling and spouting of whales and porpoises, attract them'.
CHRIS BROWN

Even where woodland existed, there was little attempt to protect or manage it. The coppiced woodland that formed part of the 150 acres of wood said to have existed on Ulva in the 1770s is one of the few Hebridean references to coppiced woodland. A 1733 memorial of abuses on the Macdonald estate, a property covering numerous touns on the eastern side of Skye, makes it clear that uncontrolled grazing by cattle over winter meant that farmers 'scarce ever allow any stick to grow bigger than what serves for a withy or for makeing creels which are much used'. So scarce was timber of any thickness on Skye that its farmers were said to use the oak and Scots fir that they dug out of peat mosses, but this use of bog timber for both building and lighting was not confined to the island by any means. For their more substantial timber needs, many Hebridean communities were given rights of wood leave on the mainland. Tenants on Harris, for example, were allowed so many boatloads of hazel and birch from the MacLeod estate's woods in Glenelg, whilst tenants on Tiree had similar access to woods in Morvern. Even an island like Lismore relied on wood leave, its tenants having access to the oak and birch woodland in Kingarloch.

On the mainland, woodland cover would have been far more extensive to start with, but even here, work on pollen samples from

Rothiemurchus Forest

Rothiemurchus Forest, a remnant of the once more extensive Caledonian Forest.

peat bogs suggest that phases of clearances had already created some pockets of open landscape by the time of Somerled. However, pollen analysis at sites along the western seaboard shows that the most significant phase of clearance was that which occurred during the two or three centuries after 1100, the time of the medieval climatic optimum when farming communities throughout Europe expanded. The scale of clearance accomplished during this period probably produced the kind of open landscape that we see today, with localised rather than extensive stands of oak and birch in the west, particularly alongside the lochs that fretted the coast, and stands of Scots pine and birch as we move east into the central Highlands. Some areas, such as Loch Arkaig, combined both types of wood, with stands of oak on its northern shore and Scots pine on its southern shore. One estimate is that by the seventeenth and eighteenth centuries, the scale of forest cover overall was down to about 20 per cent across the region. Indeed, the idea of a great Caledonian Forest extending right across the Grampians and surviving down to the early modern period has no basis in reality. It had already been heavily fragmented and localised by the end of the medieval period, though it was to be further reduced, perhaps to barely 5 per cent of total land cover, by the nineteenth century.

The increasing scarcity of timber on the mainland as the medieval period progressed meant that its exploitation, whether for ploughs, cas-chroms, roof couples, or wicker work, was closely regulated. Local court records provide frequent reference to those caught infringing by-laws on timber use. These regulations are likely to have become more stringently enforced over time as other demands were made on timber. One response to the growing shortage of timber would have been the expansion of coppicing, with its harvesting of new growth on a rotational basis. Coppicing was sufficiently widespread in the eighteenth century around the southern and eastern edges of the Highlands to suggest that it had long been practised. It demanded close control of stock, especially animals like goats, to prevent them from grazing out new growth.

By the eighteenth century, however, surviving woodlands and forests were being put under pressure from other uses. Many oak and even birch woodlands were used as a source of bark for tanning. Locally more significant, the eighteenth century saw the building of charcoal-burning iron furnaces, first beside Loch Fyne, and later at Bonawe. These furnaces depended on a supply of charcoal produced from woodlands beside Lochs Etive and Awe, supplemented by charcoal from as far away as Mull. Worked on a 20-year cycle, neither coppicing nor barking was a threat to such woodland. Indeed, by giving woodland an enhanced value within the estate economy, it helped to preserve them, but it did restrict their use. The same cannot be said of other pressures. Reports that some woodlands were fired

Lorn Furnace, Bonawe, Argyll
A charcoal-burning blast furnace built in 1753 by a group of Lake District ironmasters.

after the '45 so as to remove cover for fugitives had some basis of truth, such as in Morvern, but it was not a significant factor. More serious, at least in the southern Highlands and eastern Grampians, was the sale of large areas of Scots fir for building purposes, such as when all the timber in the barony of Grandtully in Perthshire was sold with 'free passage on the River Tay for transport' in 1724. Large amounts of timber were also moved out of the forests in Strathspey and Badenoch during the eighteenth century, floated down the Spey in the form of deals, planks, logs and spars.

Highland Travel

Travel across the Highlands and Islands was always a challenge, all the more so when we consider the practical difficulties that confronted movement prior to the modern period. Few had cause to move in any regular way across the region, and those long- distance routeways that did emerge reflected political realities, connecting major centres of political and legal authority such as Inveraray in Argyll with the Lowlands. Locally, recognised routeways would have linked estate centres with their outlying properties, but this would always have been a more difficult intercourse for wholly land-based estates than for Hebridean estates, with an estate like that held by MacLeod of

MacLeod being far-flung but reachable by sea when the weather was right. An extensive but land-locked estate like the Sutherland estate had to cope with more difficult lines of communication in reaching its outlying corners. This was partly solved by using one or two of its Assynt tenants as 'runners' to relay documents and information to Dunrobin Castle (the earl's, later the duke's, seat)when required. Ultimately, one's security as a traveller lay in the authority of the person in whose service one was travelling. Feuding and thieving during unsettled periods could make travelling hazardous for all travellers, no matter in whose service or interests they were travelling. When, during the opening decades of the seventeenth century, such thieving overlapped with the early years of the droving trade, and when cattle and the cash raised by them were being moved back and forth from some of the most remote corners of the Western Isles, travelling brought extra risks. The term 'blackmail' originated at this point to describe the money paid for protecting such cattle and cash movements from theft.

An attempt to solve the communication problems of the region, but an attempt driven by the strategic need to move troops in and out of it rather than by the growing need to market produce, was made after the 1715 Jacobite rebellion, when a number of military roads, such as the Great North Road to Inverness, were constructed by General Wade. When Cumberland's troops had to retrace the same routes after the '45 though, they were impeded by the lack of bridges even on these military roads. The lack of bridges had always been a problem. Some clan chiefs with large retinues reputedly had a *gille-casfluich*, that is a servant to carry them across the rivers!

Those early travellers to the region who have left accounts of their visit relied on a combination of hospitality provided by local tacksmen and landholders together with the comforts or otherwise of local inns or changehouses. During their tour of 1772, Dr Samuel Johnson and James Boswell experienced the full range of Highland hospitality in the pre-modern age, from their stay with MacLean of Lochbuie, a Falstaffian figure of 'hereditary consequence', to the hazards of local inns. At Glenelg, their horses were put to grass, but the inn had 'not a single article that we could either eat or drink' and the room they were shown had 'a variety of bad smells' and someone already asleep in the bed! Even by the time they toured the region, though, the demands being placed on accommodation were changing. Adding a new expectation were what the Sutherland estate called 'sportsmen', primarily those who came to fish for game fish, but, increasingly, including those who came to shoot wildfowl, grouse and deer. What had been the privilege of chiefs and their families was now seen as a commercial asset for an estate, something that could be leased out. Even by the mid-eighteenth century, fishing rights were being leased to companies, and shooting rights were also being let on a commercial basis.

On the Eve of the Clearances

Though the '45 uprising and its failure at Culloden is widely regarded as a turning-point in the history of the region, the point at which its independence of mind and behaviour finally gave way to the authority of the centre, the Highlands and Islands had already been experiencing significant change for over a century. The decades that followed the '45 saw a quickening of change, and new pathways along which it ran, but they did not initiate change. Different parts of the region experienced change in different ways.

Signs of Change

Even by 1600, many parts of the southern, eastern and northern Highlands had become involved in marketing produce as landholders fell under the influence of urban markets to the east and south, drawn not just by what they could sell to them, but also by what they could buy from them. Some of the larger estates around the Lowland-facing edges of the Highlands possessed substantial amounts of productive land, arable as well as grass. The Breadalbane estate, for instance, boasted fertile grain-producing lands in areas like Lawers and Netherlorne, as well as fertile pastures on the lower slopes of Ben Lawers and across the Braes of Balquhidder. An estate like that of Cromartie could offset the barrenness of its western portions in Coigach with the productiveness of areas like Cromartie itself and Strathpeffer that were capable of shipping out grain easily. In the medieval period, the owners of such estates would have uplifted vast quantities of food rents that they would have used to build status. But even when we start to see the workings of such estates in any detail, during seventeenth century, many had started to use the produce of their lands differently. Instead of consuming it conspicuously in the pursuit of status, we find them looking to market it. Their command over such large quantities of food rents enabled them to redirect the surpluses of the township economy, effectively adding a strong commercial component to the township's ongoing subsistence needs.

Though we have few details of this transition, it was a relatively straightforward process of change, with landowners perceiving the way in which their food rents could be revalued via the market. Many along the Highland edge were already interacting freely with Lowland society by the end of the medieval period and would have been aware of the expanding market opportunities of the early modern period. Their response is strikingly illustrated by the way grain began to flow out of the Highlands. The scale of flow involved is shown by what was marketed from the Caithness estate. Even by the mid-seventeenth century, the amount was such as to encourage the Earl of Caithness to invest in a new port at Staxigo, where he built a warehouse that reportedly could hold 4000 bolls of bere and the same quantity of oats. It was used a by number of estates to ship grain down to the towns of east-central Scotland. Further south, the Cromartie estate too became involved in the grain export trade, with records for the late seventeenth century showing the estate selling large quantities of oats and bere through merchants in Inverness.

By the sixteenth century, estates close to the Highland edge also began to sell stock. A unique set of late sixteenth-century records available for the Perthshire section of the Breadalbane estate provides a glimpse of how such estates were starting to organise their livestock economy. Like other Highland estates, the Breadalbane estate kept the stock that it had traditionally gathered in as rent at a farm known as a bowhouse. By the 1580s and 1590s, it had extended this concept to a number of townships. It used these townships to develop an estate-wide stocking policy for itself, providing cattle for the tenants and, in return, taking some of the calves and produce as rent. The stock accumulated in this way provided the estate with a regular flow of marketable beasts and produce. However, at this stage, the growing market for cattle did not affect the balance of stock kept on touns, or the way in which touns used their arable. Most still maintained a balanced mix of sheep, cattle, horses and goats. It was not until the early eighteenth century, and the surge of market prices following the Union with England (1707), that we find touns responding by adjusting their stocking balance. Signs of such a shift can be seen in parts of Lochtayside by the second quarter of the eighteenth century, with some touns starting to specialise in cattle.

The extent to which landowners around the southern and eastern edges of the Highlands sent grain and stock to market during the seventeenth century owed much not only to their greater awareness of market opportunities, but also to their growing need of money and their growing appetite for what money could buy. Some began to enlarge their castles and homes, and to bring in new costly furnishings and art works. Yet for some Highland chiefs, it was still an ambivalent world that mixed wholly different values. Thus, the seventeenth-century Campbells of Glenorchy (later Breadalbane) still maintained feuds that served their interests, such as their longstanding feud with the MacGregors. But, on the other hand, they had started to adopt different forms of behaviour and display that now depended on how well they capitalised their estate resources in cash terms. Traditional payments that might have been discharged in kind, such as for masonry work or the payment of bride-price, were increasingly settled in cash. More and more, they moved in a world that relied on cash. Arguably, long before the '45, the lifestyles of many landowners in these southern and eastern areas had locked them economically into the south even if they were not yet locked politically.

Subsistence versus Profit

When we look at what was happening further west, we find a different pattern of change. Traditional values and traditional forms of behaviour survived longer in the west. Following the collapse of the Lordship of the Isles in 1493, parts became lawless. Even allowing for the greater volume of state documentation that now becomes available for the region and the over-reaction of the state to what it saw, the sixteenth century was a time of rampant feuding between clans. This eruption of feuding was partly fuelled by the abuse of the longstanding custom of *cuid-oiche*. In the lawless conditions of the sixteenth century, men with only a marginal link to the chief's household took advantage of the custom, forcing food out of tenants. More serious, broken men, those without a clan and, as a consequence, beyond easy reach of the authorities, were forcing themselves onto tenants, an abuse known as *sorning*. These broken men were of particular concern to the authorities because they used sorning as a means of livelihood and petty feuding as a pastime.

In what became known as the 'daunting of the west', the Crown pursued a range of solutions to the perceived problems of the area. On the one hand, it tried to gain greater control by confiscating land and assigning it to more trusted landowners. This was how the Earl of Argyll acquired, first, areas like Kintyre and Knapdale, then later, Tiree, Morvern and parts of Mull. On the other hand, the Crown tackled the problem through legislation. When it began to assert its authority over the more unsettled parts of the region in the years that followed the collapse of the Lordship, the Crown outlawed sorning through local courts and eventually banned it by an Act of Parliament. But the problems afflicting the region required a more general solution. This was provided by the Statutes of Iona (1609). The Statutes curbed the practices that underpinned the lifestyle of chiefs, particularly those surrounding feuding and feasting. They restricted the number of 'household' men who could be supported by chiefs, and reduced the amount of spirits that could be stored by them. In an effort to control what it saw as 'idelmen', or those without direct means of livelihood, they outlawed sorning and bound even chiefs to work for a living. The Statutes did not have an immediate effect and what have been described as their second edition was issued in 1613 when a number of chiefs were called to Edinburgh and new conditions imposed on them. Amongst the most important was the requirement that they should levy a regular rent on their estates and pay Crown rents.

The Tacksman's House, Unish, Skye
The tacksman's house at Unish, on the exposed northern tip of Waternish, was built in the eighteenth century by the tacksman who held the Ten Pennyland of Unish from MacLeod of MacLeod.

The Statutes (1609, 1613) forced landowners in the far west into a different relationship with their estates. They had to establish regular rents and find a different way of using the large quantities of grain and stock now gathered in as rent rather than consumed as hospitality. Their approach to the latter differed from that adopted by landowners to the east. Though some continued to gather in rents in kind, especially grain payments, most landowners in the far west responded by slowly converting their rents in kind into cash rents. On the face of it, this meant it was the ordinary tenant who had to confront the problem of marketing produce in order to raise these cash rents, and who had to bear the costs of taking grain and stock to market. How they responded was to have far-reaching effects for the area. Most chose to market what walked itself to market: stock. It was a case of marketing the produce of what was abundant, grazings, as opposed to that of what was scarce, arable.

Within a decade or so of landowners being forced to rethink how they rented their properties, we find droves of cattle moving out of the region, even from the far west. What is striking about this trade as it developed over the seventeenth century is that whilst some specialist stock producers were involved, a high proportion involved small farmers contributing one or two beasts to the local cattle drove. Alongside the flow of cattle from the numerous small runrig tenants in the region, there was also a supply of beasts from touns that were farmed solely by a tacksman, using hired labour. All the signs are that tacksmen quickly became involved in cattle droving, acting as organisers of droves both for their own interests and those of the local area. In some cases, such as in Assynt, there was a contrast between different areas, the larger inland touns becoming specialist cattle farms and the coastal runrig townships remaining as arable-dominated touns but supplying one or two beasts to the local cattle drove. In other cases, it was a more localised contrast between adjacent touns, one heavily tenanted and the other functioning as the consolidated holding of a tacksman.

Tacksmen also gained from being collectors of rent. During the first half of the eighteenth century, rents rose strongly in response to a surge in the cattle trade. Tacksmen took advantage of the fact that it was far easier for them to alter the rents of those who held land beneath them than it was for their own rents to be changed. If we want to understand why many tacksmen in the far west began to build substantial two-storey stone-set houses over this period, then the answer lies not only in the profits which they gained directly from the cattle trade, but also, in the increased rents that they now gathered in as tacksmen without having to pay more rent themselves. This is what contemporary commentators meant when they talked about tacksmen beggaring those beneath them and intercepting the advantage due to those above them.

Life for the Highlander on the Eve of the Clearances

When eighteenth-century land surveys commented on the economy of the western seaboard and islands, they stressed the role of cattle as the region's prime product. In fact, this misrepresented the toun economy. What these surveys were really saying is that cattle were the main export of the region and, therefore, the prime source of cash for rents. However, when we look at how the toun economy used cattle, we find a different picture. Whilst there were some touns that could be described as specialist stock farms by the late seventeenth century, the majority still remained dependent on what their arable produced. Indeed, analysis of the Highland diet suggests that the part played by meat, if not by cheese and butter, actually declined over the late seventeenth century. Yes, stock were still important for the manure that they provided for arable, but what mattered most in the household equation of the many lesser tenants who dominated the farming landscape was the output of their arable. When landowners like MacLeod of MacLeod and the Captain of Clanranald began converting grain renders into cash payments, it enabled farmers to shift the rent burden away from arable onto grass and to consume even more of their arable output as subsistence. By the late seventeenth century, when these trends had become well-established, the typical toun of the western Highlands and Islands had effectively become polarised around a subsistence arable economy and a commercialised pastoral economy. There are signs that many touns, especially those who could use seaweed as manure, were prepared to sacrifice the one for the other. They not only ploughed or dug up green pasture for arable, but also cut it freely for turf, a practice that produced the acres of 'skinned land' to be found in parts of the Outer Hebrides. This produced what we can see as a paradox. Despite the growing number of stock that left the region for the markets at Crieff

Lazy Beds

Lazy beds were constructed by cutting two lines of turf on either side of what was to be the rig and turning them in towards the centre of the rig. The rig itself was further enriched by the addition of a range of manures depending on location: animal dung, compost, old thatch, peat, turf, seaweed, shell sand. The effect was to create a raised cultivation bed but at the expense of land in between the rigs. The term lazy bed was probably used to describe such rigs because only a portion of the land was actually in cultivation, though, in actuality, a great deal of labour was required in their construction. The farmer here is using a cas-chrom to cultivate a lazy bed. Despite its archaic appearance, there is no archaeological evidence to suppose that the cas-chrom was of great antiquity. The use of the cas-chrom, like that of the spade, required more labour than the horse-drawn plough but it rewarded farmers with a higher level of yields, an appealing trade-off in a society in which margins of subsistence were always tight.

CHRIS BROWN

Seaweed as Manure
Seaweed was used extensively throughout
the Hebrides as a manure.
NATIONAL MUSEUMS OF SCOTLAND

and Falkirk, what concerned the numerous small farmers
most was how they could expand their arable output.

Using Dr Webster's survey of 1755 as a base-line, it is
clear that many parts of the Highlands and Islands
experienced strong population growth over the second
half of the eighteenth century and that this encouraged
more emphasis on arable subsistence. As this happened,
many touns along the western seaboard and across the
Hebrides were led down a cul-de-sac of growth that
depended on high inputs of labour and allowed little
flexibility for alternative strategies of agricultural development. These
inputs relied on what was increasingly abundant, namely labour, to
sustain what was critical but scarce, arable. At the heart of these
strategies of intensification was a cultivation complex based on the use
of the spade and cas-chrom, the building of lazy beds and the
application of heavy quantities of manure, such as livestock dung,
seaweed and turf. Though these techniques are traditionally seen as
symptomatic of the archaism of the region's culture, we must not
overlook the fact that they are tools or techniques that required heavy
inputs of labour. They provided a yield bonus when compared to the
plough, but required greater amounts of labour. For this reason, they
are likely to have been used only when labour was abundant and
when communities needed to raise farm output at any price. These
two trends go hand in hand, with the smaller holdings that developed
during population growth being less able to sustain a horse plough but
more able to provide the labour needed for the spade or cas-chrom.

Such techniques suited a particular ecology of use. The cas-chrom
and spade enabled more difficult ground to be cultivated. Lazy beds,
too, enabled cultivation to be pushed out over ground that was steeply
sloping, waterlogged, covered by thin or stony soils, or broken by
rock outcrops and lochans. Used together, such techniques supported
a substantial increase in cultivable land. When the geologist J.R.
Macculloch visited the Hebrides in 1799, he described what he saw as
'almost Chinese'. The corrugated landscape of lazy beds that clothed
many steep hillsides and waterlogged soils must have been uppermost
in his mind.

Alongside such techniques of cultivation, we can find techniques of
harvesting and grain processing that were equally simple. On Skye, for
instance, many communities harvested their bere by hand, pulling it up
at the roots. Once harvested in this way, they prepared the grain by
burning away the chaff and much of the straw by a technique known
as *graddaning*, leaving them with a dry but charred grain that made
bread with all the marks of how it was made in its taste. Not surprisingly, when landowners became concerned about raising stock output,
they saw graddaning as a waste of valuable straw and set about outlaw-

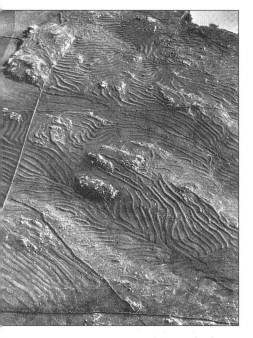

Lazy Beds, Lewis
Lazy beds enabled farmers to cultivate
difficult ground on which soils were too
thin or waterlogged, or whose cultivable
soils were broken by rock outcrops.
AEROFILMS LTD

ing its practice by the opening decades of the eighteenth century.
Once the grain was separated from the chaff, most farmers on Skye, as
in other parts of the Hebrides, then used the rotary or hand quern to
grind it.

The growing pressure on resources that was apparent by the mid-
eighteenth century provides the context in which Highland touns
adopted the potato. It was first grown in the Uists in the late 1720s, but
was not extensively grown until after 1750. The success of the potato
rested on its ability to provide 2½ times the dietary support from one
acre of arable as grain and from its ability to flourish in wet, acid soils.
Overnight, the tightly drawn bounds that restricted arable were loos-
ened, as communities used potatoes to push cultivation onto more
marginal and difficult land. In practice, it meant that people could live
off less, enabling families to survive on a mere tablecloth of arable.
People could now plant potatoes on land previously considered too
wet or acidic for oats. As the growing of potatoes spread rapidly during
the second half of the eighteenth century, communities came to rely
on them for as much as 80 per cent of their diet. As more land was
cropped and holding size fell, the Highlands and Islands became a more
crowded landscape, with pockets of acute land pressure in areas like
Assynt and Skye.

The Highlands Recorded

In the aftermath of the '45, both government and landowners
responded to the problems of the region by trying to define them in a
more exact way. By the Annexing Act of 1752, those charged with
taking part in the rebellion had their estates confiscated and put under
the control of a Board of Commissioners who were to manage them
'for the Purposes of civilizing the Inhabitants'. The Forfeited Estates,
as they were called, covered a range of property from the Struan estate

Lazy Beds, Europie
Lazy beds at Europie, on the northern tip of
Lewis.

in Perthshire to the Knoydart estate on the west coast opposite Skye. The Commissioners, mostly Lowlanders or English with an outsider's perception, saw their future as one of improved farming. They achieved some success on estates in Perthshire, enclosing land and introducing fodder crops like turnips and sown grasses, as well as laying out a new village for craftsmen at Kinloch Rannoch, but their hope of having such ideas diffuse more widely was optimistic. In time, it was the rising market for sheep that brought widespread change, not the Commissioners.

One of the Government's responses to the '45 was an attempt to better understand the region. Its search for better information operated in different ways. At a local level, the Commissioners for the Annexed Estates carried out systematic surveys of the estates under their control. The survey of the Knoydart estate, one of the most marginal estates in the whole of the western Highlands, was especially detailed. It documents the limited patches of arable available to touns sited along the north side of Loch Nevis and south side of Loch Hourn, their cropping and stocking, the labour intensiveness of their husbandry with cas-chroms and querns used throughout the estate, and the severe nature of their setting. Indeed, so severe was their setting that many touns reported a loss of stock each year by 'bone break' as stock were moved to the shieling over ground that was steep and dangerous.

At a larger scale, a detailed cartographic survey of the Highlands was initiated under Major-General William Roy, 1747–55. Commissioned by the Duke of Cumberland in the immediate aftermath of Culloden, and carried out from 1747 onwards, the Roy

Skiary in Knoydart

Back in the eighteenth century, Skiary was a typical Knoydart toun on the south side of Loch Hourn, small in size and marginal in character. William Morison's survey of 1771 described it as occupied by two tenants. Between them, they farmed three acres of arable on the loch side, cropping only oats, using a spade or cas-chrom and manuring with seaweed. In addition, they kept sixteen cows plus a 'few sheep'. They were banned from keeping goats because of the damage caused to the regeneration of birch and Scots pine on the slopes that lay behind the toun. In all probability, this was a recent ban. What struck Morison most was the fact that the farm had 'a most horrid appearance from the steepness of the hill and numberless impending rocks, which threaten destruction to every creature, and bring on great losses to the tenants by the death of their cattle occasioned by falls from the rocks'.

The ANATOMIE of the PARISH & BARONY of Ardnamorvchan and Swinard.

NAMES of the TENEMENT	Families	Men	Women	Children	Examinable	No of Acres on each Tenement	Cowes	Horses	Sheep	Pounds	Shillings	Pence	Cheese	Butter	Sheep	Cheese	Butter	Sheep	Kids	Veal's	Pounds	Shillings	Pence	Bolls	Firlots	Pounds	Shillings	Pence	Pounds	Shillings	Pence	Pounds	Shillings	Pence	NATURALL AND UNCOMMON PRODUCT	Woods
Terbart	4	6	6	10	22	3	2700	54	10	54	8	15				3	3	1	3	3	3	3				6	3					5	12	1¾	Woods, Shell sand, Freestone, Iron Ware, Corn, Cattle, Fish, Fowl	18000
Laga	7	13	8	11	32	5	4050	90	16	90	10	2	10	5	5	1	5	5		3	3	10	5									8	4	15	2	Woods, Excellent Whin-Stone, Sea Ware, Corn, Cattle, Fish, Fowl	
Glenbarrodale	6	9	13	11	33	5	2400	90	20	90	9		6	5	5	1	4	4	2	2	2	10	5		2	2	1	2	2	8	4	13		Woods, Shell sand, Iron Ware	
Glenbeg	9	9	11	15	35	4	1670	56	12	56	5		4	4	1	4	4	2	2	2	8	4	1	3					6	8	9		Some Woods, Shell sand, Sea Ware, Shell sand	800
Glenmoir	5	9	7	13	29	5	1360	60	16	60	5		1	4	4	1	4	4	2	2	8	4	1	1					8	4	10		Some Woods, Sea Ware, Shell sand	
Ardflignifh	5	10	8	14	32	5	1800	60	16	60	6			5	5	1	5	5	2	2	10	5							8	4	14	9	Shell sand, Sea Ware	
Camisangaall	9	13	13	35	5	1110	72	18	72	9	14		6	6	1	6	6	2	2	2	12	17		2	3	15		10	16	3	4	Shell sand, Sea Ware	
Tornamoany	5	9	6	4	19	4	780	48	12	48	5			4	4	1	4	4	2	2	8	4	1	3					6	8	9	6	Sea Ware	
Bourblaige	7	9	11	15	35	5	650	60	16	60	7	7		5	5	1	4	4	2	2	10	5	2	2	1	2		8	4	12	3	Sea Ware, Vaine of Talck	
Skinad	9	12	14	20	46	5	1480	60	16	60	6	5		5	5	1	4	4	2	2	10	5	3	1	1	8		8	4	11	7	Limestone, Marble, Slate	
Coriuolline	7	9	11	9	29	6	1350	72	18	72	8	11		6	6	1	5	5	2	2	12	7	3	1	1	8		10	14	7		Wood, Shell sand, Sea Ware, Lime, Corn, Iron Ore, Copper Ore	
Mingary	8	13	11	4	28	6	1700	96	24	96	13	6		8	6	1	5	5	2	2	12	7	5	1	2	6	8	10	20			Sea Ware, Marble, Iron Ore	
Kilchoan	8	13	12	10	35	5	1080	60	16	60	6	5		5	5	1	4	4	2	2	10	5	3	1	6	8		8	4	11	5	Shell sand, Iron Ore, Lime Stone	
Ormsaigmoir	6	9	8	12	29	4	984	48	12	48	5			4	4	1	4	4	2	2	8	4	3	1	1	8		6	8	9	13	Sea Ware, Marble, Iron Ore	
Ormsaigbeg	6	8	10	10	28	5	1640	60	16	60	7	7		5	5	1	4	4	2	2	10	5	2	1	1			8	4	12		Sea Ware, Lime Stone, Iron Stone, Marble	
Girgadale	5	9	8	7	24	5	1960	60	16	60	7	7		5	5	1	4	4	2	2	10	5	2	2	1	2		8	4	12	3	Sea Ware, Shell sand, Pearl	
Achahofnich	6	9	14	11	34	9	2000	108	30	108	12	7		8	8	2	7	7	3	3	18	9	6		2	13	4	15	21	5		Some Woods, Shell sand, Sea Ware	
Achnaha	5	9	10	14	33	5	1365	60	16	60	6	5		5	5	1	4	4	2	2	10	5	2	2	1	2		8	4	11	3	Woods, Sea Ware, Shell sand	
Glendrien	6	6	8	15	29	5	2220	48	16	48	5	2		5	5	1	4	4	2	2	8	4	1	3				15	6¾	8	4	Sea Ware, Pearl	
Falkadale	2	3	3	3	9	3	3050	126	36	126	18			9	9	2	9	9	4	4	18	9	7		3	2		15	28	5		Some Woods, Shell sand, Sea Ware	
Achateny	10	17	21	17	55	6					1		2				9	9	2	9	9	4	4	18	9	7					Some Woods, Sea Ware, Shell sand	
Braynanault	8	7	12	12	31	5	500	60	16	60	9	5		5	5	1	5	5	2	2	10	5	3		1	6	8	8	4	14	10	Woods, Some Sea Ware	
Kilmorri	6	10	10	8	28	4	1100	108	27	108	12	7		8	8	2	8	8	4	3	18	9	6		2	13	4	15	21	12		Sea Ware, Limestone	
Swardilchonach	6	9	9	6	24	5	780																								Sea Ware, Lime Stone, Marble	
Swardilmoir	5	10	6	8	24	5	1230	60	15	60	6	5		5	5	1	4	4	2	2	10	5	3		1	6	8	8	4	11	5	Sea Ware, Wood	
Swardilchoul	9	14	12	11	37	8	2340	96	25	96	12	15		8	8	2	7	7	3	3	16	8	3	1	1	8		13	4	20	5	Sea Ware, Woods	1200
Gortonfern	3	5	5	4	14	1	875	16	3	16												½					1	1½	1	8	1	19	Sea Ware, Woods	
Lehick					1		875	16	3	16				1			1	1		1	1		2	1		½			1	1½	1	8	1	19	Woods	
Clath & Ardrimnifh	2	4	7	2	13	2	1750	32	6	32	2	10		2	2	1	2	2	1	1	4	2		1		2	2½	3	4	4	5	Woods, Shell sand, Sea Ware	
Daal and Gortenoorn	8	12	12	19	43	6	2980	96	15	96	10	16	8	6	6	1	4	4	2	2	12	7	1	1¼		12	2½	10	15	11	4	Woods, Shell sand, Sea Ware	16760
Ardtoe & Watterfoot	4	8	11	9	28	6	2000	64	12	64	6	2	2	4	4	1	4	4	2	2	8	4		2		4	5	6	8	9	11	Woods, Shell sand, Sea Ware, Salmon Fishing	8060
Acharakle	9	10	14	19	43	5	3380	80	15	80	9		6	5	5	1	4	4	2	2	10	5	1	2		13	4	8	4	13	7	Woods, Freestone, Shell sand	20096
ARDNAMORCHAN	201	292	314	351	957	152	55050	2016	489	2016	244	17	2	148	148	33	132	132	62	62	62	16	16	8	82	2½	36	14	5½	12	13	4	395	3	0		74916

'The Anatomie of the Parish and Barony of Ardnamurchan and Swinard' compiled by Sir Alexander Murray of Stanhope in 1727.

or Military Survey as it became known provided the first large-scale survey of the region, one that provides a detailed inventory of the landscape, including settlement, arable, woodland, and enclosures. Even allowing for the inaccuracies in Roy's map, we get, for the first time, some sense of how land uses were proportioned and how settlements and arable were laid out. It depicts a largely open landscape, one that shows far more arable than can be seen today, but with far fewer enclosures. The other feature that stands out is the paucity of forest or woodland. By the mid-eighteenth century, the southern Highlands were already a relatively naked landscape.

In the decades that followed, the number of detailed surveys compiled by estates grew dramatically, as landowners realised that in order to capitalise on their estates, they first had to draw up an inventory of what was present. Written surveys, such as that compiled in 1727 by Sir John Riddell for his Arnamurchan and Sunart estate, had been available for some time, but not in cartographic form. By the mid-eighteenth century, the cartographic survey had become an essential part of estate management. In some cases, their fine-scale detail enables us to reconstruct the traditional landscape of the region before it disappeared under sheep and crofting. Whilst there are exceptions from the Northern Isles, and in the case of one or two touns on the edge of the eastern Highlands, we rarely see the runrig layout of touns in these surveys, for, as a temporary arrangement between tenants, runrig had no permanent significance for a toun. However, many plans depict the layout of arable in graphic detail and, in some cases, the ordering of the toun in terms of infield–outfield, meadow and common pastures, together with the disposition of farmstead, kailyards, storehouses, and the like. Where plans are sufficiently detailed, what is striking about the layout of mid–late eighteenth century arable is its irregular and highly fragmented layout, many touns having numerous small, detached pieces of arable. Of course, what they cannot convey is the labour-intensive techniques by which such plots were cultivated. In some cases, we are faced with an almost garden-like farm landscape, one in which great effort and care were being expended for each acre of subsistence wrought from the land.

Though estate plans depict settlement, they do not always do so reliably. Where plans were surveyed more precisely, we can learn something about the general disposition of settlement, its location relative to arable, but many touns, especially in the west, present a complex mix of house sites. This is confirmed by surviving field evidence for eighteenth-century settlement. Part of this complexity stemmed from the changes experienced by ordinary peasant housing across the eighteenth century. The small oval-shape house plans evident in parts of the Hebrides at the start of the century gave way to larger, more rectangular plans, 5–6 metres long by the middle decades of the century. Such shifts in house size were ongoing, for by the early nineteenth century, we find croft dwellings whose length was as much as 20–25 metres, usually with a byre incorporated at one end. Similar shifts in house size are evident on the mainland. Longhouse sites surveyed in the Braemar area suggest a similar scalar increase in the

The Macdonald Estate, Skye
An extract from Mathew Stobie's 1766 plan of the Macdonald estate on Skye. Stobie, a Lowland surveyor, surveyed the extensive lands of the Macdonald Estate in the 1760s, producing two maps, one in 1764 and the other in 1766.
CLANDONALD LANDS TRUST

A Pre-Improvement Landscape
The daugh or davoch of Deskie, Glen Livet, showing its pre-Improvement landscape, 1761.
NATIONAL ARCHIVES OF SCOTLAND

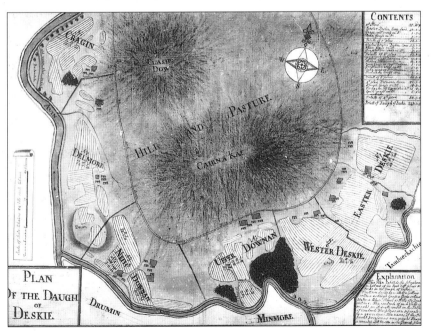

eighteenth century, with the more recent forms having more rectangular as well as larger ground plans. A fully excavated site at Lianach near Balquhidder in Perthshire, one dated to the eighteenth century, was measured as 20 metres in length. We can also begin to discern more clearly the regional variation in house types, at least amongst those with dry-stone walls, with some having gable ends and others hip-ended roofs, some having a low wall and the roof rising from the inner edge whilst others had roofs that overhung the outer wall edge.

Change and the Clearances

By the mid-eighteenth century, the Highlands were being subjected to pressures that, ultimately, were to bring about far-reaching changes that were radical in their effects and all-embracing in their extent. For the vast majority of small farmers, the old field economy of oats and bere provided a livelihood that hovered all too easily around the margins of subsistence whilst yielding an uncertain rent for the landowner. Despite the colonisation of more arable and an increasing use of the potato, the population growth of the eighteenth century accentuated these problems by the closing decades. Alongside these increasing problems in the old Highland economy, though, were critical changes in the market opportunities now open to Highland farming. Following the Union in 1707, the market for stock rose sharply. At first, the Highlands responded by increasing the flow of cattle. What had been a modest but steady stream of stock now became a vigorous flow. But by the 1750s, the market advantage in so far as the Highland farmer was concerned shifted to sheep. Starting in 1754, when a farm on the Luss estate beside Loch Lomond was cleared, estates began to respond to this burgeoning demand for sheep by clearing runrig touns and their arable-oriented economy and replacing them with a sheep-based farm economy, sometimes putting two or three runrig touns together in the process. By doing so, landowners were able to increase their rents 200–300 per cent and to reap the benefits of a more certain rent, but only at the cost of dispossessing a tenantry that had farmed its fields and hills for centuries. As it unfolded over the closing decades of the eighteenth century, Highland history was driven by the collision between these two trends: the increasing number of small farmers and the growing inadequacy of their farm economies on the one hand and the expanding market and profitability of sheep farming on the other. Landowners resolved the problem in one of two ways. They either cleared runrig touns to make way for sheep or, the solution widely adopted in the north and west, they reorganised touns into crofting townships, either *in situ* or on what invariably was poorer land nearby. Whatever solution was adopted though, it brought a distinct era of Highland history to an end and an equally distinct phase in its landscape history.

How Do I Find Out More?

The Highlands and Islands have an abundance of archaeological sites surviving from the medieval period. They include a wide range of ecclesiastical buildings, from St Mary's abbey at Iona to the remains of simple twelfth-century chapels, from elaborate standing crosses to equally ornamental grave-slabs. Strongholds also abound, from early castles of enclosure that were continually elaborated over the medieval and early modern periods, and which are still inhabited today, to castles that saw little elaboration and were abandoned by the end of the medieval period. Though we know less about them, many ordinary peasant settlements have also survived in some abundance. Recent surveys, including richly-detailed landscape surveys carried out by the Royal Commission on the Ancient and Historical Monuments of Scotland (RCAHMS), have highlighted just how many traces of ordinary peasant settlements have survived in the landscape, from concentrations of dwellings and outbuildings beside their former arable to shieling sites on their hill pasture. Some have survived in such detail as to require little imagination to repeople them in the mind.

Sites marked HS are opened to the public by Historic Scotland.

Sites to See

Argyll and Bute

Bonawe, Taynuilt, Argyll. Charcoal-burning blast furnace, erected in 1753. The Bonawe furnace relied on coppiced wood from surrounding woodlands, both beside Lochs Etive and Awe and from Mull. (HS) NN 009318

Castle Stalker, Appin. A 16th-century tower house inhabited by the Stewarts of Appin. NM 920473

Castle Sween, Argyll. A late 12th-century castle of enclosure. Abandoned in the 17th century. (HS) NR 713789

Finlaggan, Islay. Finlaggan consists of two small islands at the east end of Loch Finlaggan. It was a key site for the Lordship of the Isles. Situated on one of the two islands was the residence of the Lord of the Isles, as well as his chapel. The other, known as Council Isle, was occupied by the hall in which the Council of the Lordship met, as well as by other contemporary buildings. Recent excavations have shown that Council Isle was also the site of an earlier 13th-century castle and, at a still earlier date, an Iron Age dun, suggesting that it had long been a focus of lordship. NR 388681

Iona. St Mary's Abbey, Nunnery and St Oram's Chapel Buildings, as well as crosses and grave-slabs. (HS) NM 287244, NM 287245 and NM 284240

Keills, Mid Argyll. Medieval chapel, with examples of late medieval monumental sculpture. (HS) NR 690806

Mingary Castle, Ardnamurchan. A 13th-century castle of enclosure built on a small rock outcrop beside the shore. It underwent internal changes down until the 18th century. NM 502631

Oronsay Priory, Oronsay. The remains of a late 14th-century Augustinian priory, founded with the help of the Lord of the Isles. NR 349889

Grampian

Glen More Forest. Surviving remnants of the native Highland pine forest can be seen in a number of areas. That at Glen More, near Aviemore, and that at Rothiemurchus, a few miles to the west, are two of the more easily accessible. NH 980090, NH 920080

Upper Dee valley, Braemar area. The remains of former shieling sites occur on hill ground across the region, mostly between 300 and 500 metres. Examples can be found along the upper part of the Dee valley, part of the Mar Lodge estate. NO 000855 to NO 046894

Perthshire and Kinross

Glen Shee. A relatively well-preserved former landscape of pre-Clearance and pre-Improvement dwellings, outbuildings and kailyards, as well as associated cultivation rigs, can be seen extending along the Glen from the church at Spittal of Glenshee to Dalmunzie. NO 109701 to NO 092709

Balquhidder. The area beside Loch Voil, running west of Balquhidder, was once part of a royal hunting forest, and actively used by the Crown as such during the 15th century. NN 536207

Ross and Cromarty

Foulis Rent House, Ross and Cromarty. Built in the mid-18th century as a storehouse for grain gathered in from the estate owned by the Munros of Foulis. NH 599636

Ullapool, Wester Ross. A planned fishing village based on fisher-crofts laid out in 1788 by the British Fisheries Society. The grid plan of the village is still clearly evident. NH126944 to NH 127939

Skye and Lochalsh

Armadale, The Clan Donald Centre. The Clan Donald centre provides much information for the history of a major Highland clan grouping, the clan Donald. NG637043

Eilean Donan Castle, Lochalsh. Built in the 14th century. The relatively unmodified main hall at Eilean Donan Castle illustrates the sort of hall in which chiefly feasts would have taken place. NG882258

Unish, Watternish, Skye. Tacksman's house, tenant houses and enclosures at the northern tip of Waternish. NG 239658

Sutherland

Strathnaver, Sutherland. Cleared by the Sutherland estates in 1814, the abandoned sites of some of its former touns can be seen at Grumbeg and Grumore on the north bank of Loch Naver, at Bas an Leathaid and at Rosal. NC 634384, NC 608367, NC 701360, NC 689416.

Western Isles

Arnol, Lewis No 42, restored blackhouse. (HS) NB 310494

Barvas, Lewis. The damage caused by the extensive removal of turf for building purposes, the underlying soil for manure and peat for fuel or manure, led to skinned land, which simply means land without any turf or soil cover. Examples can be seen inland from the crofting townships that lie along the north-west coast of Lewis, from Barvas to South Dell. NB 364502

Bragar, Lewis. Remains of the pre-crofting toun at Bragar, including rigs, enclosures, house footings and outbuildings, can be found close to the shore. As with other touns along the north-west coast of Lewis, their pre-crofting settlement was located closer to the shore. NB 293488

Europie, Lewis. Lazy beds. The most north-westerly toun in the Hebrides. The northern part of the former toun contains some of the finest examples of surviving lazy beds in the region. NB 522658

Illeray, Benbecula. Abandoned pre-1700 house platforms and house sites. The toun of Illeray was devastated by storms in the 1690s and again in the mid-18th century. Its former house platforms now lie amidst tidal creeks and flats. NF 786636

The Udal, North Uist. Site of a medieval and early modern toun. A large and complex settlement mound on a peninsula at the tip of North Uist. Its excavation revealed a succession of settlement from prehistory down to the late seventeenth century, when the farming toun on the site was abandoned. NF 820780

Museums

The region has a wide range of regional and local museums and heritage centres, as well as numerous clan centres. Those most relevant to the themes covered in his book include The Highland Folk Museum (Kingussie and Newtonmore), the West Highland Folk Museum (Fort William), Auchindrain Township Open Air Museum (Furnace, Argyll), and the new Museum of the Isles (Armadale). Local museums of particular interest include No 42, Arnol (Lewis), Glencoe and North Lorn Folk Museum (Glencoe, Lochaber), Laidhay Folk Museum (Caithness), Kilmuir (Skye), and Strathnaver Museum (Bettyhill, Sutherland).

Further Reading

Aberdeen and North-East Scotland, Exploring Scotland's Heritage series, I A G Shepherd (HMSO 1996 edition)

Argyll and the Western Isles, Exploring Scotland's Heritage series, G Ritchie and M Harman (HMSO 1996 edition)

The Buildings of Scotland: Highlands and Islands, J Gifford (Penguin 1992)

Clanship, Commerce and the House of Stuart, 1603–1788, A I Macinnes (Tuckwell Press 1996)

From Chiefs to Landlords, R A Dodgshon (Edinburgh University Press 1998)

Lost Kingdoms. Celtic Scotland and the Middle Ages, J L Roberts (Edinburgh University Press 1997)

The Kingdom of the Isles. Scotland's Western Seaboard

c.1100–c.1336, R A MacDonald (Tuckwell Press 1997)

The Highlands, Exploring Scotland's Heritage series, J Close-Brooks (RCAHMS 1986)

The Island Blackhouse, and a Guide to 'The Blackhouse' No 42, Arnol, A Fenton (Historic Scotland 1989 edition)

The Northern and Western Islands of Scotland: Their Economy and Society in the Seventeenth Century, F Shaw (John Donald 1980)

North East Perth. An Archaeological Landscape (RCAHMS 1990)

Waternish, Skye and Lochalsh District, Highland Region, Afforested Land Survey (RCAHMS 1993)

HISTORIC SCOTLAND safeguards Scotland's built heritage, including its archaeology, and promotes its understanding and enjoyment on behalf of the Secretary of State for Scotland. It undertakes a programme of 'rescue archaeology', from which many of the results are published in this book series.

Scotland has a wealth of ancient monuments and historic buildings, ranging from prehistoric tombs and settlements to remains from the Second World War, and HISTORIC SCOTLAND gives legal protection to the most important, guarding them against damaging changes or destruction. HISTORIC SCOTLAND gives grants and advice to the owners and occupiers of these sites and buildings.

HISTORIC SCOTLAND has a membership scheme which allows access to properties in its care, as well as other benefits. For information, contact: 0131 668 8999.

THE AGE
OF THE CLANS